Building Wealth, Indian Style: A GUIDE TO FINANCIAL FREEDOM

Transform Your Money Journey with Smart Investments

SANJAY KUMAR SINGH

INDIA • SINGAPORE • MALAYSIA

ISBN 979-8-89632-908-4

To my Mother and Father,
whose unwavering support and timeless lessons on hard work, discipline, and perseverance
have shaped me into who I am today.
To my beloved wife, Rasmi Singh,
whose constant encouragement and belief in me
inspire me every day to pursue our dreams together.
To my daughter, Shreya Singh,
whose curiosity and innocence remind me to keep striving
for a better future, not just for me, but for you.
This book is dedicated to all those seeking financial freedom
and a brighter tomorrow.

Contents

Preface

Thank you for picking up this book. I truly hope the ideas shared here help you as much as they have helped me and so many others. My biggest wish is that this book makes a positive difference in your life and helps you create the future you dream with financial freedom by building wealth. Welcome to **Building Wealth, Indian Style: A Guide to Financial Freedom** — your ultimate guide to navigating the world of investing and building wealth, tailored for young Indian investors but with timeless principles that anyone, anywhere, can use to achieve financial freedom. Whether you're just starting out or looking to take your financial journey to the next level, this book will provide you with the knowledge and tools to transform your financial future.

In India, as in many parts of the world, the landscape of personal finance is changing rapidly. The traditional methods of saving — like relying solely on fixed deposits, savings accounts, or physical assets such as gold — are no longer enough to create lasting wealth. Today, young people are looking for smarter ways to grow their money and build financial security, even as global markets and technologies evolve. The question isn't just *how* to save, but *how* to invest in a way that makes your money work for you.

This book is designed to bridge that gap — to introduce you to the world of investments, explain foundational principles, and show you how to use these tools to build wealth and achieve financial independence, no matter where you're from.

Here's what you can expect to learn from the chapters ahead:

- **Building a Strong Financial Foundation**: We start with the basics, focusing on how to budget, track your expenses, and create a financial plan that allows you to save and invest. You'll learn simple but powerful techniques for organizing your finances and making every rupee (or dollar) count towards your goals.
- **The Power of Compounding**: Compounding is one of the most powerful forces in personal finance, and it works the same way whether you're in Mumbai, New York, or London. This book will help you understand how to leverage compounding to grow your wealth over time, no matter how much or how little you start with.
- **Investing Smartly, Starting Small**: Investing isn't reserved for the wealthy — it's for anyone with the right knowledge and discipline. Whether you're investing in Indian equity markets, international funds, real estate, or stocks, this book will show you how to start small, diversify, and grow your portfolio with confidence. Topics include mutual funds, stocks, SIPs (Systematic Investment Plans), real estate, and more.
- **Achieving Financial Independence**: Inspired by the global FIRE (Financial Independence, Retire Early)

movement, you'll learn strategies tailored for India, but easily applicable anywhere. We'll explore how to eliminate debt, maximize your savings, and create passive income streams that enable you to reach financial independence — the freedom to live life on your own terms, without being tied to a paycheck.

- **Managing Risk and Market Volatility**: All investments come with risk, and markets go through cycles. This book explains how to assess your risk tolerance, manage market volatility, and stay calm during financial storms. With a focus on long-term strategies, you'll learn to make decisions that help you weather uncertainty and stay on track with your goals.
- **Maximizing Tax Savings**: In India and across the world, taxes are a significant consideration when planning investments. You'll learn how to use tax-saving instruments like PPF, NPS, and ELSS to minimize your tax burden, while simultaneously growing your wealth. Understanding tax-efficient investing is key to building a larger corpus for your future.
- **Real-World Case Studies**: Along with actionable advice and easy-to-follow steps, we'll look at real-life examples — from young professionals in India to entrepreneurs and investors worldwide — to understand how others have successfully built wealth and achieved financial freedom.

This book is not just a manual for getting rich; it's a roadmap to financial security, independence, and the freedom to live life without financial constraints. While the specific tools and investment options may vary depending on where you live, the core principles — budgeting, saving, investing, and building passive income — apply universally.

The path to financial freedom isn't a sprint; it's a marathon. By starting early, staying disciplined, and making informed decisions, you can reach your goals. No matter your starting point, financial independence is achievable.

The strategies in this book are designed with India in mind — but they are equally relevant to anyone, anywhere in the world, who is seeking financial freedom. Whether you live in a bustling Indian metropolis or a small town, whether you're an aspiring tech professional, a small business owner, or simply someone looking to create a better financial future, you'll find practical tips and strategies that work.

As you read this book, keep in mind that financial freedom is a journey. There will be challenges along the way, but with the right knowledge and mindset, you can overcome them and come out stronger. Let this book be your guide as you take that first step toward a life of financial independence, where your money works for you, not the other way around.

Let's get started — your financial freedom begins today.

What This Book Will Do For You

This book is a heartfelt guide designed to help you achieve your financial dreams. It's more than a manual; it's a trusted companion on your path to financial security and freedom, offering practical strategies to grow and manage wealth in every major asset class.

Build a Strong Foundation on Investment

Simplify Investing in Indian style

Explore Modern Investment Options

Achieve Financial Freedom

Save Smartly on Taxes

Harness the Power of Compounding

Master Real Estate Investments

Make Confident Choices in investment

Above all, this book is about empowering you to live the life you deserve. It's not just about money—it's about freedom, security, and building a future full of possibilities for you and your loved ones.

Let's get started — your financial freedom begins today.

1

Investing Essentials for Young Indians: Building Wealth from Scratch

Ravi and Priya, a young couple in their late 20s, were full of dreams and eager to build a bright future. Ravi worked as a software developer, and Priya was a school teacher. After their wedding, they moved to a bustling city, excited about the opportunities it offered.

Despite their steady incomes, they were often puzzled by their empty savings at the end of each month. "Where does all our money go?" Priya wondered one evening. The wake-up call came when a car repair bill drained their small savings. "What if something bigger happens?" Priya said with concern.

Ravi agreed, "We need to get serious about our finances."

That night, while browsing online, Ravi found a book: *Building Wealth, Indian Style: A Guide to Financial Freedom* by **Sanjay Kumar Singh**. Intrigued, they decided to give it a try.

"This is exactly what we need," Ravi said. And so, their journey toward financial independence began.

Step 1: Understanding Personal Finance

The first chapter of the book taught them the importance of budgeting. They sat down together and started tracking their income and expenses, dividing their spending into three categories:

1. **Needs**: Essentials like rent, groceries, and utility bills. Priya noted a powerful quote:

> *The lack of money is not the problem. The problem is how you think about money."*
>
> *– Robert T. Kiyosaki*

2. **Wants**: Dining out and subscriptions were adding up quickly. They decided to cut back, limiting dining out to one special dinner each month.
3. **Savings/Investments**: They realized they had never saved seriously and decided to start an emergency fund covering three to six months of expenses. Ravi called it their "financial safety net."

Step 2: Setting Financial Goals

"Let's set clear goals to stay motivated," Priya suggested. They outlined three goals:

- **Short-Term**: Build an emergency fund within six months.
- **Mid-Term**: Save for a vacation to the hills next year.
- **Long-Term**: Buy their dream home in five years.

To make it achievable, they broke these into smaller steps. For example, they decided to save ₹10,000 a month to reach their emergency fund goal in six months.

"Every big dream starts with small steps," Priya said with a smile.

Step 3: Learning About Investments

One Sunday, Ravi's friend, an investment advisor, visited. Over tea, they discussed money management.

"Budgeting is a great start," the friend said, "but savings alone won't help you grow wealth. You need to invest."

He explained the benefits of mutual funds and SIPs (Systematic Investment Plans) , Stocks, ETF, Bond , Tax rules, and other investment instruments and how compounding could exponentially grow their money over time.

"It's like planting a tree," he said. "The earlier you start, the bigger it grows."

That week, Ravi and Priya opened their first SIP account, feeling both excited and confident.

Step 4: Staying Disciplined

Over the next few months, their financial habits began to pay off. Their emergency fund grew steadily, and their investments started showing returns.

However, a sudden medical expense tested their resolve. This time, instead of panicking, they used their emergency fund and avoided debt. They replenished it the following months.

Small milestones, like saving ₹50,000, were celebrated with simple joys like homemade pizza or a movie night. "Discipline is tough, but it's worth it," Ravi reflected.

One Year Later: Sharing Their Success

A year later, Ravi and Priya invited friends over and shared their journey.

"Start small, but start today," Priya said. "Building an emergency fund gave us peace of mind, and setting clear goals kept us on track."

"It's not about how much you earn but how you manage it," Ravi added, quoting Sanjay Kumar Singh's advice: *"It's not how much money you make that makes you rich; it's how much money you keep."*

"Ravi and Priya's story isn't unique. Many young couples and individuals face similar challenges when managing their finances. The good news? It's never too late to take charge. Let's begin with the basics of personal finance and then understand how to build wealth to get a financial freedom and learn how to build a strong financial foundation."

Understanding Personal Finance Basics

Personal finance is the foundation of any investment journey. It's about managing your money wisely to build a strong financial base for future investments.

Budgeting: Keeping Track of Your Money

Budgeting is a key financial practice that can help anyone take control of their money, avoid wasteful spending, and achieve long-term financial freedom. When done right, budgeting ensures that your money works for you, rather than you working for your money. Let's dive deeper into this essential step towards financial independence.

Tracking Income and Expenses

To start budgeting, you first need to have a clear understanding of how much money is coming in and how much is going out each month.

- **Income**: This refers to the total money you earn from all sources. This could be your salary, business profits, rental income, dividends, interest, etc. Understanding your income is the first step to creating a budget.
- **Expenses**: These are all the things you spend money on. Expenses can vary greatly from one person to another, so it's crucial to categorize them accurately. Regularly tracking your expenses will give you a better idea of where you are overspending and where you can cut back.

Dividing Your Expenses into Three Categories

It's helpful to break down your expenses into three categories to make things clearer. This makes it easier to evaluate if you are spending money wisely and staying aligned with your financial goals.

- **Needs (Essentials)**

  These are unavoidable expenses that are necessary for your survival and day-to-day living.

  - Examples include:
- Rent or mortgage payments
- Groceries and food
- Utilities (electricity, water, internet)
- Transportation costs (fuel, bus fare, car EMI)

- Insurance premiums (health, life, etc.)
  - These are non-negotiable, and while you can reduce costs here (by moving to a cheaper place or cutting down on consumption), they must be budgeted for every month.

Wants (Discretionary Spending)

These are non-essential items that you can live without but might enjoy.

- ➢ Examples include:
- ➢ Dining out, ordering food
- ➢ Entertainment (movies, concerts, subscriptions to streaming platforms like Netflix)
- ➢ Hobbies (traveling, expensive gadgets)
- ➢ Fashion (clothes, accessories)

- While these are important for enjoying life, they are areas where you can reduce spending if necessary to save or invest more.

Quote by Morgan Housel:

"Rich people buy assets. Poor people buy liabilities."

- ➢ **Savings/Investments (Future Planning)**

  This is money that you put aside to achieve long-term goals, such as buying a house, retiring comfortably, or investing for wealth-building.

- Examples include:
  - ➢ Setting aside money for an emergency fund

- Contributions to retirement plans like EPF (Employees' Provident Fund), PPF (Public Provident Fund), or NPS (National Pension Scheme)
- Investment in mutual funds, stocks, bonds, gold, or real estate

- It's crucial to prioritize savings and investments, as this is what will help you build wealth and financial security over time.

Quote by Brian Tracy:

"The key to financial freedom and great wealth is a person's ability to convert earned income into passive income or portfolio income."

Quote by Shiv Khera:

"Winners don't do different things, they do things differently."

Why Budgeting is Key to Financial Freedom

Many people earn money but struggle to build wealth because they don't keep track of their income and expenses. Effective budgeting helps you create a clear path toward achieving your financial goals.

- **Prevents Overspending**: By categorizing your spending into needs, wants, and savings, budgeting helps you avoid impulse purchases and unnecessary expenses.

- **Promotes Saving**: Having a budget forces you to allocate money to savings and investments regularly, ensuring that you're building wealth for the future.
- **Improves Financial Control**: A budget gives you control over your money, allowing you to decide where every rupee should go, instead of letting it slip away through careless spending.

The Role of Interest Rates and Regulations in Budgeting

Be aware that certain financial factors, such as interest rates and government regulations, can impact your budget and investment strategy.

- **Interest Rates**:
  - Interest rates directly affect the cost of borrowing money. For example, if you have loans (e.g., home loan, personal loan), higher interest rates mean you will pay more in EMIs each month. Conversely, lower interest rates make borrowing cheaper.
  - Interest rates on savings accounts and fixed deposits can also change yearly. Be sure to keep an eye on any changes from banks or financial institutions that could affect your savings or investments.
- **Government Regulations and Taxes**:
  - Tax rates change from year to year, and new financial regulations might impact your investment options. For instance, tax-free income limits or changes to the tax treatment of investment returns (such as capital

gains tax or dividend tax) can affect your overall budget and financial planning.

Quote by Napoleon Hill:

"A goal is a dream with a deadline."

Quote by Robert T. Kiyosaki

"It's not how much money you make that makes you rich, it's how much money you keep, and how hard it works for you."

Setting Financial Goals: How It Helps and How to Do It

1. **Provides a Purpose and Motivation to Save:**
   - **Why Goals Matter**: Goals are the reasons behind your savings and budgeting. When you have specific goals, it becomes easier to resist unnecessary expenses and stay on track.

   Examples of Common Goals:
   - **Buying a Home:** A long-term goal like purchasing a home gives you a big reason to save.
   - **Education Fund:** This could be for your education or your child's future studies, especially if you're thinking of expensive options like college or specialized training.
   - **Retirement:** Planning for retirement early can help ensure you have a comfortable life when you stop working.

- **Benefit:** Clear goals help you see the big picture and remind you why you're managing your money carefully.

2. **Makes Your Goals Specific, Measurable, and Time-Bound:**
   - **Set Clear and Specific Goals:** A general goal like "I want to save money" is less effective than a specific goal, such as "I want to save ₹5 lakhs in the next 3 years for a down payment on a house." The more specific the goal, the easier it is to track your progress.
   - **Set Timeframes for Each Goal:** Adding a timeline to your goals makes them measurable. For example:
   - **Short-Term Goals (within 1 year):** Buying a new gadget, taking a vacation, or creating an emergency fund.
   - **Mid-Term Goals (1-5 years): Saving for a car, a wedding, or a home down payment.**
   - **Long-Term Goals (5 years or more):** Saving for a child's college fees, building retirement savings, or buying a house.
   - **Trackable and Realistic:** Specific, time-bound goals help you measure progress and adjust if needed. If you set a realistic timeline, you're more likely to achieve your goal.

3. **Break Down Large Goals into Smaller Steps:**
   - Why Breaking Down Helps: Big goals like buying a house or saving for retirement can feel overwhelming.

Splitting them into smaller steps makes them more achievable.

Example of a Savings Goal for a House:

- Decide on a target amount, e.g., ₹10 lakhs for a down payment.
- Decide how much you can save each month, e.g., ₹10,000.
- Calculate how long it will take, e.g., saving ₹10,000 each month will take about 8 years to reach ₹10 lakhs.
- Adjust as Needed: If the timeline feels too long, consider increasing your monthly savings if possible. Small steps help you see progress and stay motivated.

4. **Helps Prioritize Your Spending and Saving:**
   - Identify Essential vs. Non-Essential Expenses: With goals in mind, it's easier to identify what's worth spending on. Ask yourself if an expense is helping you get closer to your goal or if it's a distraction.
   - Make Trade-offs to Save More:
   - Instead of eating out frequently, maybe you cook at home more often to save for that vacation you've been planning.
   - Small sacrifices today can lead to bigger rewards tomorrow, like a more comfortable retirement or a fully paid home.
   - Focus on High-Priority Goals First: If you have multiple goals, prioritize them based on importance. For instance, an emergency fund might be your first

goal, followed by saving for retirement or a down payment on a home.

5. **Boosts Your Motivation and Discipline with Money**
Building strong financial habits often requires motivation and discipline. Staying committed to your budget and financial goals can be challenging, but tracking progress, setting clear milestones, and rewarding yourself can keep you motivated along the way. Let's explore how these practices can help you stay on track and build long-term wealth.

Seeing Progress Encourages More Saving

When you track your progress toward a financial goal, it creates a sense of achievement, which can significantly boost your motivation.

- **Visualizing Progress**: When you can see how far you've come, whether it's through a savings tracker, an app, or even a simple chart on your wall, it reminds you of the progress you're making. The feeling of being closer to your goal makes the effort feel worthwhile.
    - **Example**: If you're saving for a vacation and you know that you've already saved ₹50,000 out of your ₹100,000 target, you'll be more likely to continue saving because you can see that you're halfway there. This visibility makes it easier to stay motivated and stick to your budget.
- **Positive Reinforcement**: Every time you make progress, it reinforces the idea that your discipline is

paying off. When saving becomes a habit, it becomes easier and more rewarding to stay on track.

Quote by Brian Tracy:

"*The act of setting a goal is not as important as the act of achieving it.*"

Monthly or Quarterly Check-Ins

Checking your progress regularly—either monthly or quarterly—helps ensure that you're on track to meet your financial goals. This allows you to make adjustments as needed and reinforces your commitment to your financial plan.

- **Reviewing Your Budget**: At the end of each month, check how much you've saved versus how much you planned to save. If you're behind, take corrective action—perhaps you need to cut back on certain "wants" or shift money from one goal to another. Regular reviews keep you accountable and help you avoid drifting away from your objectives.
- **Adjusting Your Plan**: Life is unpredictable, and sometimes, you may face unexpected expenses or income changes. Monthly or quarterly check-ins help you assess if your budget still makes sense and whether you need to adjust your strategy (e.g., saving a little more, cutting back on discretionary spending).
  - **Example**: If your initial plan was to save ₹5,000 a month for an emergency fund, but after three months you realize that you've only managed ₹3,000 per

month, your quarterly review helps you identify where you're falling short. You can then plan to save ₹7,000 per month for the next three months to catch up.

Quote by Shiv Khera:

"You do not rise to the level of your goals, you fall to the level of your systems."

Celebrating Milestones

Celebrating small wins along the way is a great way to maintain motivation and make the journey toward financial freedom more enjoyable.

- **Small Treats for Achievements**: When you reach a financial milestone, such as saving your first ₹10,000 or hitting the halfway mark of your emergency fund target, treat yourself in a way that doesn't sabotage your progress. For example, you might reward yourself with a small, budget-friendly treat like a nice meal out or a movie night.
- **Psychological Boost**: Celebrating milestones provides a sense of accomplishment and positive reinforcement. It reminds you that each step you take brings you closer to your larger financial goals.

Quote by Napoleon Hill:

"What the mind of man can conceive and believe, it can achieve."

The Power of Motivation and Discipline in Achieving Financial Freedom

Building wealth requires patience, discipline, and ongoing motivation. By staying focused on your goals, regularly reviewing your progress, and celebrating small victories along the way, you'll build a positive financial habit that can lead to long-term success.

- **Long-Term Consistency**: It's not about big, one-time sacrifices or sudden bursts of saving. It's the daily, consistent efforts that add up over time. The more you track your goals, celebrate milestones, and make adjustments as needed, the more disciplined you become in managing your money.
- **Avoiding Burnout**: Motivation often wanes when progress seems slow or distant. By celebrating smaller milestones and checking in with your budget regularly, you stay energized and less likely to experience burnout or frustration.
- **Sustaining Momentum**: Motivation is a renewable resource. The more progress you see and the more milestones you celebrate, the more momentum you'll have to continue pushing toward your financial goals.

Quote by Robert T. Kiyosaki:

"The most important thing is to be able to make decisions that lead to financial freedom. You'll never reach your goals if you can't make the right choices along the way."

6. **Helps You Make Informed Financial Decisions:**
   - **Smart Choices:** When you know what you're working towards, you're less likely to spend on things that don't matter.
   - **Avoids Impulse Purchases:** Having goals makes you think twice about impulse buys, as you'll know that money could go toward something meaningful.
   - **Increased Financial Confidence:** Working toward goals builds financial confidence. You'll know that each decision you make is bringing you closer to something you genuinely want or need.

Putting It All Together: A Practical Example

Imagine you're 25 and want to buy a house by 35. Here's how you might plan:

1. Set the Goal: Save ₹20 lakhs for a down payment.
2. Make it Specific and Time-Bound: "I'll save ₹20 lakhs over 10 years by saving ₹16,700 per month."
3. Track Progress: Check every 3 months to see if you're on track. Adjust if necessary.
4. Stay Motivated: Remember the freedom and stability owning a home will bring.
5. Adjust Spending Choices: Skip unnecessary shopping sprees or limit eating out to keep saving.

Setting financial goals doesn't just help you build wealth—it gives your money direction, helping you achieve what matters most to you in life.

Absolutely, let's dive even deeper into tracking tools and how they can transform budgeting into a powerful way to manage and grow your finances. Here's an expanded breakdown:

Financial Discipline: Building Good Money Habits for Long-Term Wealth

Financial discipline is the practice of managing your money wisely and making smart decisions to build wealth over time. It involves avoiding unnecessary debt, developing saving habits, and being consistent with your financial goals. Here's a deeper look at how to achieve and maintain financial discipline:

1. **Avoiding Unnecessary Debt**
   - Understand the Cost of Debt: Not all debt is harmful, but certain types, especially high-interest debt like credit card loans, can quickly become overwhelming and costly. High-interest rates mean that even small debts can grow rapidly, making it harder to pay off.
   - Limit Credit Card Usage: Only use credit cards if you can pay off the balance each month. This avoids interest charges and keeps your credit score healthy.
   - Avoid 'Buy Now, Pay Later' Traps: While it can be tempting to finance purchases over time, this can lead to more debt than you planned for. It's best to save up and pay in full whenever possible.
   - Think Before Borrowing: Ask yourself if the debt is necessary and if it will help you achieve a financial goal. For example, a home loan or student loan might be a positive debt because it contributes to long-term

goals, whereas credit card debt for non-essential items usually doesn't.

2. **Building a Habit of Saving**
   - Pay Yourself First: One of the simplest and most effective saving habits is to "pay yourself first." This means setting aside a portion of your income for savings as soon as you're paid, rather than waiting to see what's left at the end of the month.
   - Start Small if Necessary: If you're new to saving, start with a small, manageable amount, like 10% of your income. You can increase this amount as you get comfortable with the habit.
   - Automate Your Savings: Set up an automatic transfer from your checking account to your savings or investment account each month. Automation ensures consistency, and you'll build savings without thinking about it.
   - Emergency Fund First: Prioritize saving for an emergency fund (3-6 months of living expenses) before putting money into other investments. This fund acts as a financial cushion, preventing you from needing loans or credit cards in emergencies.
3. **Practice Delayed Gratification**
   - Think Before Spending: Financial discipline means resisting the urge to buy things impulsively. Before making a purchase, give yourself time to consider whether it's a "need" or a "want." Often, you'll find that waiting a day or two reduces the urge to buy.

- Set Aside for Big Purchases: If you want something costly, like a new gadget or vacation, plan and save for it rather than buying on credit. This builds patience and prevents unnecessary debt.
- Reward Yourself Thoughtfully: Financial discipline doesn't mean you can't enjoy your money. Set aside a small amount for personal enjoyment each month, but avoid going overboard.

4. Consistent Investment for Wealth Building

- Invest Regularly: Even small, regular investments grow over time due to compounding. Setting aside a portion of your income to invest each month builds long-term wealth.
- Use SIPs (Systematic Investment Plans): SIPs allow you to invest a fixed amount in mutual funds regularly. This "dollar-cost averaging" approach reduces the risk of timing the market and helps you grow your investments steadily.
- Monitor and Adjust: Financial discipline includes reviewing your investments periodically and adjusting as needed to stay on track with your goals.

5. Stay Committed to Your Financial Goals

- Review Your Progress: Check in on your budget, savings, and investment goals regularly—monthly or quarterly. This will help you see your progress and make any adjustments to stay on track.
- Avoid Lifestyle Inflation: As income increases, it can be tempting to increase spending. Practicing financial

discipline means keeping your lifestyle relatively steady and putting extra income towards savings and investments.

- Celebrate Small Wins: Reward yourself for meeting financial milestones, whether it's saving a specific amount or staying debt-free for a year. This positive reinforcement strengthens your commitment to financial discipline.

The Importance of Emergency Funds: Your Financial Safety Net

An emergency fund is one of the first and most essential steps in financial planning. Before beginning any serious investment, it's important to establish this fund, as it serves as a financial safety net, protecting you in times of unexpected crises. Emergencies, like sudden medical bills, urgent home repairs, or even job loss, can lead to unplanned expenses. Having an emergency fund ensures that such events don't derail your financial stability.

Let's dive deeper into the why, how, and where of building an effective emergency fund.

1. **How Much to Save: Building a Reliable Cushion**
   - **The 3-6 Month Rule:** Most financial experts recommend saving enough to cover 3 to 6 months' worth of essential living expenses. This includes basic costs like rent or mortgage, groceries, utilities, insurance, and any mandatory bills.

- **Determining Your Exact Needs:** Your exact emergency fund target depends on your unique financial situation.
- **If You Have Dependents:** For people with dependents (such as children or elderly family members), it's often safer to aim for the higher end of the spectrum (6 months or more). Dependents rely on you, so this extra buffer ensures their needs are also met.
- **For Freelancers and Self-Employed Individuals:** If your income is unpredictable or varies month to month, you might want to save even more (6 to 12 months' worth of expenses) to protect yourself during low-income periods.
- **Dual-Income Households:** If you're part of a dual-income household where both partners work, you might opt for a smaller fund (closer to 3 months). However, having at least 3 months' expenses is still essential, as a second income can serve as backup in case of job loss.

2. **Where to Keep It: Accessible and Low-Risk Options**

   Since the purpose of an emergency fund is to be easily accessible, it's best kept in safe, low-risk places where you can withdraw the money quickly without penalties. Here are some of the most suitable options:

   Savings Account:

   - **Quick Access:** A savings account allows you to access your funds immediately, either by online transfer or ATM withdrawal.

- **Safety:** Savings accounts are one of the safest places to keep money since they're insured by banks.
- **Low Interest:** While interest rates are generally low compared to other investments, savings accounts are meant for liquidity, not high returns. The primary purpose here is ease of access.

Liquid Mutual Funds:

- **Slightly Higher Returns:** Liquid mutual funds invest in short-term, low-risk debt instruments. While they carry slightly more risk than a savings account, they often yield higher returns, which can help your emergency fund grow.
- **Quick Redemption:** Most liquid funds allow you to withdraw your money within 24 hours without significant penalties, giving you quick access in emergencies.
- **Ideal for Those Seeking Growth:** If you want your emergency fund to grow a bit faster while remaining relatively low-risk, liquid mutual funds can be a good option.

Fixed Deposits (FDs):

- Security and Higher Interest Rates: FDs are popular for their safety and higher interest rates compared to savings accounts.
- Flexibility for Premature Withdrawal: While fixed deposits are meant to be held until maturity, many banks offer the option to withdraw early, often with a small penalty.

- Laddering Strategy: To maintain access to funds without locking everything away, you can "ladder" your FDs by opening multiple accounts with different maturity dates. This ensures that you have access to a portion of your funds at regular intervals without incurring penalties.

3. **Purpose of Emergency Funds: The Do's and Don'ts of Using It**
   - Only for True Emergencies: The emergency fund should be strictly reserved for unexpected, essential expenses that impact your well-being or financial stability. These may include:
   - Medical Emergencies: Hospital bills, medication, or surgeries that aren't covered by insurance.
   - Job Loss: Income replacement for necessities while you search for a new job.
   - Home or Car Repairs: Urgent repairs that affect your safety or ability to commute (e.g., a broken-down car or severe water leakage in your home).
   - Not for Luxuries or Non-Essential Spending: Vacations, shopping sprees, or entertainment expenses shouldn't be funded by your emergency reserves. Using your fund for these purposes can leave you vulnerable in an actual emergency.
   - Self-Control Is Key: It can be tempting to dip into this fund, especially if you see it as easily accessible cash. Financial discipline is crucial to ensure that

your emergency fund remains untouched until a real need arises.

Why an Emergency Fund Matters

An emergency fund not only protects you from the financial stress of unexpected events but also offers peace of mind. Knowing you have a safety net reduces anxiety about "what if" scenarios. With an emergency fund, you won't have to resort to high-interest credit cards, loans, or pulling out investments in a hurry, which can lead to heavy penalties or disrupt your long-term financial goals.

Having an emergency fund is like owning insurance for your finances: it's there to protect you when the unexpected happens, allowing you to make level-headed decisions instead of scrambling for funds.

Introduction to Investing: Growing Wealth for the Long Term

Investing is the process of using your money to buy assets—such as stocks, bonds, or real estate—that have the potential to grow in value over time. It's one of the most effective ways to build wealth, achieve financial goals, and work toward financial independence. Unlike saving, which focuses on security and easy access, investing aims to increase the value of your money over time, albeit with some level of risk.

1. **Saving vs. Investing: Knowing the Difference**

   Understanding the distinction between saving and investing is essential, as they serve different purposes in financial planning.

Saving:

- Purpose: Saving is primarily for short-term needs, emergencies, or goals that require quick access to funds. Savings accounts are ideal for this, offering security and liquidity, meaning you can easily access the money whenever you need it.
- Features: Savings accounts are low-risk, as they're typically insured by banks and offer stable, if modest, interest rates.
- Returns: Interest rates on savings accounts are generally low (around 3-4% per year), which means that while your money is safe, it doesn't grow significantly.
- Example: Think of saving as setting aside funds for an upcoming purchase, like a vacation or new appliance. The focus is not on growth but on safety and accessibility.

Investing:

- Purpose: Investing is focused on wealth-building over the long term, helping you reach larger financial goals like retirement, buying a home, or funding a child's education.
- Features: Investments come with varying levels of risk, but they also offer potential for higher returns. Investing involves buying assets like stocks, mutual funds, bonds, or property that can appreciate over time.

- Returns: While returns are not guaranteed, many investments, especially stocks, offer the potential for much higher growth, often between 10-15% per year over long periods. This growth comes with risk, as the value of investments can fluctuate.
- Example: Consider investing if you want your money to grow significantly and you're willing to leave it untouched for several years, allowing it to ride out the ups and downs of the market.

2. **Potential Returns and the Power of Compounding**
   - Potential for Higher Returns: One of the main reasons people invest is to achieve returns higher than what traditional savings accounts offer. While a typical savings account might yield 3-4% annually, investments in stocks have historically provided returns closer to 10-15% over long periods, though this isn't guaranteed and comes with volatility.
   - The Role of Compounding: Compounding occurs when the returns earned on an investment are reinvested, allowing future returns to be earned on an increasingly larger base.
   - Example: Imagine investing ₹10,000 with a 10% annual return. After one year, it grows to ₹11,000. In the second year, instead of earning 10% on your original ₹10,000, you're now earning 10% on ₹11,000, so your investment grows to ₹12,100. Over time, compounding significantly increases the growth of your investment.

- Long-Term Impact: Compounding favors those who invest early and reinvest their earnings. For example, an investment of ₹1,00,000 at a 10% annual return can grow to more than ₹2,00,000 in about 7 years. The longer you let your money compound, the greater the wealth-building impact.

3. Why Investments Involve Risk and How to Manage It

Risk-Reward Tradeoff: Every investment carries a level of risk, meaning there's a chance the asset's value could decrease. However, higher-risk investments, like stocks, generally offer higher potential returns, while lower-risk investments, like bonds or FDs, offer smaller but more stable returns.

Types of Risks:

- Market Risk: This is the risk of losing money due to fluctuations in the market, often affected by factors like economic downturns, political changes, or global events.
- Inflation Risk: If the return on your investment is lower than the rate of inflation, your purchasing power decreases over time. This risk especially affects savings accounts, as they often provide lower returns than inflation rates.
- Liquidity Risk: Some investments are harder to convert into cash quickly. For example, real estate takes time to sell, making it less liquid than stocks.

Managing Risk:

- Diversification: Spreading your money across different types of assets (like stocks, bonds, and real estate) helps reduce risk. If one investment performs poorly, others may do well, balancing your overall returns.
- Investing for the Long Term: Markets are unpredictable in the short term, but they tend to grow over time. Long-term investing gives you a better chance to recover from short-term declines and benefit from growth.
- Understanding Your Risk Tolerance: Everyone has a different comfort level with risk. Knowing your risk tolerance will help you choose the right mix of assets. If you're uncomfortable with volatility, you might prefer a balanced portfolio with a mix of stable bonds and some stocks.

4. **Why Start Investing Early? The Advantage of Time**
   - More Time for Compounding: The earlier you start investing, the more time compounding has to work. Even small, regular investments can grow substantially over many years.
   - Recovery from Market Downturns: Younger investors have time on their side, allowing them to ride out market ups and downs. If the market takes a dip, they have the flexibility to wait for recovery, unlike someone closer to retirement.

- Building Wealth Consistently: Starting early creates a habit of regular investing. Even if you start with small amounts, consistent contributions add up over time and create a strong financial base.

Types of Investments: Choosing the Right Mix for Your Financial Goals

Investing is not a one-size-fits-all approach, and understanding the different types of investments can help you create a balanced portfolio suited to your financial goals and risk tolerance. Here's a closer look at some of the most common investment types.

1. **Stocks: Ownership in a Company**
   - What They Are: Stocks, also known as equities, represent a share of ownership in a company. When you buy a stock, you become a shareholder, owning a small portion of the company and sharing in its success or failure.
   - How They Work: Stock prices fluctuate daily based on factors like company performance, industry trends, and market conditions. Profits are generated through price appreciation (when the stock price goes up) and dividends (periodic payments made by the company to shareholders).

Pros:

- High Return Potential: Historically, stocks have offered higher returns over time than most other types of investments, making them a powerful tool for wealth building.

- Liquidity: Stocks can be bought and sold quickly, providing flexibility if you need to access your money.
- Dividend Income: Some companies pay dividends, which can provide a steady income stream.

Cons:

- Volatility: Stocks are volatile and can experience sharp price changes, especially in the short term.
- Risk of Loss: There's no guarantee of returns, and you can lose a portion or all of your investment if the company underperforms or the market declines.
- Best for: Investors with a long-term horizon who can withstand market fluctuations and are seeking growth over time.

2. **Mutual Funds: Professionally Managed Investment Pools**
    - What They Are: Mutual funds pool money from multiple investors to buy a diversified portfolio of assets like stocks, bonds, or other securities. Managed by professional fund managers, mutual funds are designed to achieve a specific investment objective, such as growth, income, or balanced returns.
    - How They Work: When you invest in a mutual fund, you own shares in the fund itself, rather than in the individual stocks or bonds the fund owns. The fund's performance depends on the combined performance of all the securities in its portfolio.

Types of Mutual Funds:

- Equity Funds: Invest primarily in stocks for growth potential.
- Bond Funds: Focus on fixed-income securities for stable returns.
- Balanced Funds: Combine stocks and bonds for a mix of growth and stability.

We will discuss mutual fund in details in subsequent chapter.

3. Bonds: Fixed-Income Investments

- What They Are: Bonds are essentially loans that investors make to governments, municipalities, or corporations. In exchange, the issuer pays regular interest payments and repays the principal (the original amount invested) at a set maturity date.
- How They Work: Bonds generate returns through interest payments, known as the coupon rate, which is usually fixed. When the bond matures, the investor receives the initial investment amount back.

Types of Bonds:

- Government Bonds: Issued by the government and considered very low-risk, but offer lower returns.
- Corporate Bonds: Issued by companies; they generally offer higher returns but come with greater risk.
- Municipal Bonds: Issued by states or municipalities, often with tax-free benefits for residents.

Pros:

- Predictable Income: Bonds provide a steady, predictable income stream from interest payments.
- Lower Risk: Bonds are less volatile than stocks, making them a safer investment option, especially government bonds.
- Portfolio Stability: Adding bonds to an investment portfolio can help balance the risk of stocks.

Cons:

- Lower Returns: Bonds generally provide lower returns compared to stocks, so they may not keep pace with inflation over time.
- Interest Rate Risk: Bond prices can decrease if interest rates rise, as new bonds offer higher returns, making older bonds less attractive.
- Best for: Investors seeking stable income, preservation of capital, and lower risk, especially those nearing retirement or with a low-risk tolerance.

4. Real Estate: Tangible Property Investments

- What It Is: Real estate includes physical properties, such as residential homes, commercial buildings, or rental properties. Real estate can generate income through rent or appreciate in value over time, providing returns when the property is sold.
- How It Works: When you invest in real estate, you own a tangible asset. Real estate can appreciate over time, allowing you to sell it for a profit, or generate rental income, providing a steady cash flow.

Choosing the Right Mix of Investments

Each investment type has its strengths and weaknesses. The right combination depends on factors like your risk tolerance, financial goals, and time horizon. For example:

1. Young Investors: May benefit from a higher allocation in stocks and mutual funds, focusing on long-term growth.
2. Conservative Investors: May prefer bonds or balanced mutual funds that offer more stability and income.
3. Balanced Investors: A diversified mix of stocks, bonds, and perhaps real estate could balance risk and growth.

Understanding these investment types enables you to build a well-rounded portfolio that aligns with your financial aspirations and risk tolerance, positioning you for a more secure financial future.

How to Get Started with SIPs: A Simple Guide to Regular, Long-Term Investing

A Systematic Investment Plan (SIP) is one of the easiest and most effective ways to start investing in mutual funds. By contributing a fixed amount of money at regular intervals (often monthly), you can build wealth over time while reducing the impact of market volatility. Here's a deeper look into how SIPs work and why they're an excellent choice for both beginners and experienced investors.

1. **Benefits of SIPs: Why SIPs Make Investing Easier and Smarter**

   A. Dollar-Cost Averaging (DCA):

   - What It Is: Dollar-cost averaging is a strategy where you invest a fixed amount regularly, regardless of the market conditions. This means you buy more units of the mutual fund when prices are low and fewer units when prices are high.

- How It Works:

Let's say you invest ₹5,000 every month in a mutual fund. If the unit price of the fund is ₹100 in the first month, you buy 50 units.

In the next month, if the unit price rises to ₹120, you only get 41.67 units.

Over time, this process averages out the price at which you're buying the units, reducing the impact of short-term market fluctuations and lowering the risk of investing a lump sum at a market high.

Why It's Beneficial:

- Less Timing Stress: You don't need to worry about market timing or trying to pick the best time to buy. By investing regularly, you take the emotion out of the decision-making process.
- Reduces the Impact of Market Volatility: Since markets move up and down, SIPs allow you to ride out the highs and lows, without having to predict the market's movements.

B. Compounding Power:

- What It Is: Compounding is when the returns you earn on your investments are reinvested to generate even more returns. Essentially, your money starts to make money.

- How It Works: Suppose you invest ₹5,000 per month in an SIP, and the mutual fund gives you an annual return of 12%. Over time, not only will you earn returns on your original investment, but also on the returns that have already been added to your fund.
- In other words, your earnings begin to grow exponentially as your investment generates additional income, which is reinvested and contributes further to your wealth.

Why It's Beneficial:

- Exponential Growth: The earlier you start, the more time you give your money to grow, leading to potentially significant returns over the long run.
- Long-Term Wealth Building: Compounding allows your wealth to multiply over time, especially when you invest consistently over several years.

2. Starting Early: Why Time is Your Best Friend in SIPs

A. The Earlier, the Better:

Time and Growth: The key to benefiting from SIPs is to start early. The longer your money stays invested, the more it has the opportunity to grow through compounding.

Example:

If you start investing ₹5,000 monthly at the age of 25, and you earn an average annual return of 12%, by the time you reach 60, you could accumulate a substantial amount, thanks to compounding over 35 years.

If you delay starting the SIP by just 5 years (starting at 30 instead of 25), your investment may yield significantly less, even though the monthly contribution remains the same.

Why It's Beneficial:

- More Time for Compounding: The earlier you start investing in SIPs, the more time you give your money to compound. Even small amounts invested early can grow into substantial sums over time.
- Less Impact of Short-Term Market Movements: Long-term investments in SIPs generally smooth out the ups and downs of the market, making it a safer way to invest over time.

4. Consistency is Key: Stick to Your SIP

- Stay Committed: The power of SIPs lies in consistency. Even if the market fluctuates, keep investing regularly. Over time, this will allow you to ride out market cycles and benefit from the long-term growth of your investments.
- Avoid the Temptation to Withdraw: One of the most common mistakes is withdrawing the money when markets are down or when you need the cash. Instead, stay patient, as short-term market movements are less important in the long run.

Risk and Reward: Understanding the Balance in Investing

In the world of investing, risk and reward are two fundamental concepts that go hand-in-hand. The key to successful investing is understanding these two elements and finding the right balance that matches your financial goals, time horizon, and risk tolerance.

1. **Risk: The Chance of Loss**

   Risk refers to the possibility that you could lose some or all of the money you invest. Every investment carries some level of risk, and the higher the potential for reward, the higher the risk. Here's how to understand risk in different types of investments:

   - Stock Market Risk: Stocks are generally considered high-risk investments because their prices fluctuate based on factors like company performance, market trends, and economic conditions. If the stock market or a company experiences a downturn, the value of stocks can fall significantly.
   - Bond Risk: While bonds are generally safer than stocks, they are not risk-free. The primary risk associated with bonds is credit risk, where the issuer (like a government or company) may fail to repay the principal or interest. Additionally, interest rate risk means that the value of a bond can decrease if interest rates rise.

   Example: If interest rates rise, the value of your bond may fall, reducing your potential return.

   - Currency and Inflation Risk: For international investments or long-term investments, currency fluctuations and inflation can also pose risks. Currency value changes can impact your returns if you invest in foreign assets, while inflation erodes the value of money over time.

How to Manage Risk:

- Diversify your investments across different asset classes (stocks, bonds, real estate, etc.) to reduce the impact of any single investment's poor performance.
- Regularly monitor your portfolio to make adjustments based on changing market conditions and your personal risk tolerance.

2. Reward: The Potential for Profit

Reward refers to the returns or profits you can make from your investments. In simple terms, it's the gain you hope to achieve by investing your money. The reward is often a percentage return on the amount you invested and varies by asset class:

- Stocks: Historically, stocks have offered some of the highest long-term returns, averaging around 10-15% annually. However, this comes with higher risk due to market volatility.

Example: If you invest ₹1,00,000 in stocks and the stock market has an average return of 12% per year, your investment could grow to ₹1,12,000 by the end of the year.

- Bonds: While bonds tend to offer lower returns (generally 4-6%), they are considered safer investments compared to stocks. Bonds offer fixed interest payments, providing a stable and predictable income stream.

Example: If you invest ₹1,00,000 in bonds with a 5% interest rate, you could expect ₹5,000 annually as interest income.

- Real Estate: Real estate investments can provide steady rental income and the potential for price appreciation. The reward is the combination of rental income and the property's value increasing over time.

Example: If you buy a property for ₹50,00,000, you might earn ₹10,000 in rent each month. After several years, the property may also increase in value, providing you with a capital gain when sold.

Maximizing Rewards:

- Long-term investments tend to reward you more due to the power of compounding.
- Be strategic and patient—some investments may take years to realize significant returns.

3. **Understanding Your Risk Tolerance**

When it comes to investing, risk tolerance refers to how much risk you're willing to take with your money in order to achieve your investment goals. It varies from person to person and depends on several factors like your age, financial situation, investment objectives, and previous experience with investing. Understanding your risk tolerance is key to making investment decisions that align with your comfort level and financial goals.

Let's break down the concept of risk tolerance and how to assess it:

Types of Risk Tolerance

There are generally three categories of risk tolerance—**low**, **moderate**, and **high**—each suited to different kinds of investors based on their individual circumstances.

Low Risk Tolerance

If you're cautious about losing money or if your financial goals are short-term, you might prefer to take minimal risk with your investments.

- **What it Looks Like**:
  - You prioritize stability and predictability over high returns.
  - Your focus is on preserving capital rather than seeking big gains.
  - You may prefer investments that provide regular, fixed income, such as bonds or fixed deposits, because they're considered safer and more stable.
- **Investment Options**:
  - **Bonds**: Government or corporate bonds, which offer regular interest payments and return the principal at maturity.
  - **Fixed Deposits (FDs)**: Bank FDs that provide guaranteed returns with low risk, though returns are typically modest.
  - **Debt Mutual Funds**: Mutual funds that invest in bonds or other debt securities.
- **Ideal For**:
  - People nearing retirement or those who need to access their money in the short term (e.g., within 1-3 years).

- Individuals who are not comfortable with the idea of their investment fluctuating significantly in value, even if that means sacrificing potential gains.
- Warren Buffett: "The stock market is a device for transferring money from the impatient to the patient."

➢ **What it Looks Like**:

- You're okay with some market fluctuations and understand that risk is part of investing.
- You prefer a diversified portfolio, which means investing in a mix of assets like stocks and bonds to balance risk and return.
- You want to grow your wealth over time but don't want to gamble everything on high-risk assets.

➢ **Investment Options**:

- **Balanced Mutual Funds**: These funds typically invest in a mix of equities (stocks) and debt (bonds), giving you both growth potential and relative stability.
- **Index Funds**: These are low-cost funds that track a market index, such as the Nifty 50 or Sensex, offering broad exposure to the stock market with moderate risk.
- **Equity and Debt Portfolio**: A mix of stocks and bonds, where stocks provide growth and bonds provide stability.

➢ **Ideal For**:

- People with medium-term financial goals (5-10 years) or those who have some time to ride out market fluctuations.

- Investors who can tolerate some market volatility and are willing to take on a bit more risk in exchange for potentially higher returns.

Quote by Morgan Housel:

"Risk comes from not knowing what you're doing."

High Risk Tolerance

If you have a high risk tolerance, you're willing to take on greater risk in exchange for the possibility of higher rewards. These investors are open to market volatility and understand that large gains are often accompanied by significant risk.

- **What it Looks Like**:
  - You're comfortable with the possibility of losing money in the short term for the potential of higher returns in the long run.
  - You're focused on long-term growth and willing to ride out market fluctuations.
  - You may be comfortable investing in riskier assets like stocks, real estate, or even cryptocurrencies.
- **Investment Options**:
  - **Equity (Stocks)**: Direct investments in stocks, especially in growth stocks, which can offer high returns but are volatile.
  - **Real Estate**: Investing in property, which can appreciate over time, though it comes with its own set of risks like market crashes or liquidity issues.

- **Cryptocurrency**: Emerging, highly volatile assets that have the potential for big returns but come with significant uncertainty and risk.

Quote by Robert T. Kiyosaki:

"The more a person seeks security, the more that person feels insecure."

Speaking with a Financial Advisor

If you're unsure about your risk tolerance, it's a good idea to speak with a financial advisor. They can help you assess your risk tolerance in more detail and create a personalized investment plan that aligns with your goals, timeline, and comfort level.

- **Why a Financial Advisor Can Help**:
  - They can help you understand complex investments and explain the risks involved in each asset class.
  - They can help you create a diversified portfolio that aligns with your risk tolerance, so you can avoid taking on more risk than you're comfortable with.
  - They can also help you adjust your portfolio as your life circumstances change (e.g., nearing retirement or adjusting to new financial goals).

Quote by Brian Tracy:

"Successful people are simply those with successful habits."

Understanding risk tolerance is a key step in crafting a financial strategy that works for you. Take the time to assess your comfort with risk, review your financial situation, and choose investments that align with your goals. This way, you'll be better equipped to make confident, informed investment choices on your journey toward financial freedom.

2

Navigating India's Stock Market: A Beginner's Guide to Smart Investing

How the Stock Market Works: Understanding the Basics

The stock market is a vital component of the financial system, where individuals and institutions buy and sell stocks, which represent ownership in companies. It provides a platform for companies to raise capital by issuing shares and for investors to potentially grow their wealth by purchasing these shares. Let's break down the core concepts that will help you understand how the stock market works, especially in the context of India.

Basic Terminology

1. **NSE (National Stock Exchange)**

   The **NSE** is India's largest stock exchange by trading volume, and it plays a crucial role in the Indian economy. It offers a fully automated electronic trading system, which makes buying and selling stocks quick and efficient.

- **What is NSE?**
  - The NSE is a marketplace where investors can trade shares of companies. It uses advanced technology to ensure smooth and transparent trading, making it easier for individuals and institutions to buy and sell stocks.
- **Key Index: NIFTY 50**
  - The **NIFTY 50** is the NSE's benchmark index, which represents 50 of the largest and most actively traded companies in India across various sectors. It's widely used by investors to track the overall health of the market.
- **Example**:
  - **Infosys** is a well-known technology company listed on the NSE. If you are looking to invest in the technology sector, you might track the performance of Infosys on the NIFTY 50 index. A strong performance of Infosys could indicate a positive trend in the technology sector.

Quote by Warren Buffett:

"The stock market is a device for transferring money from the impatient to the patient."

2. **BSE (Bombay Stock Exchange)**

   The **BSE** is Asia's oldest stock exchange, founded in 1875. It is one of the leading stock exchanges in India and plays a significant role in shaping the Indian financial landscape.

- **What is BSE?**
  - The BSE is another marketplace where investors can trade stocks. It's known for its rich history and has helped shape the development of the Indian stock market.
- **Key Index: Sensex**
  - The **Sensex** (Sensitive Index) is the flagship index of the BSE and includes 30 of India's largest and most influential companies. The Sensex is a reflection of the market's overall health and a key indicator of the Indian economy.
- **Example**:
  - **Reliance Industries** is one of the companies listed on the BSE and included in the Sensex. If you monitor the Sensex, you can get a sense of how large companies like Reliance are performing. A decline in the Sensex could signal a dip in the overall market, affecting companies like Reliance.

Quote by Benjamin Graham:

"The individual investor should act consistently as an investor and not as a speculator."

3. NIFTY

The **NIFTY 50** is a key index of the **NSE**, representing the 50 largest companies across various sectors in India. It's one of the most commonly tracked benchmarks for the Indian stock market and reflects the market's overall performance.

- **What is NIFTY 50?**
  - NIFTY is a broad-based index that includes companies from industries such as information technology (IT), banking, energy, FMCG (Fast-Moving Consumer Goods), and more. The performance of this index reflects the health of the stock market and economy in general.
- **Example:**
  - **TCS** (Tata Consultancy Services) is one of the companies in the NIFTY 50, representing the IT sector. When the NIFTY rises significantly, it's often driven by growth in companies like TCS, as well as other key sectors like banking, which might be represented by companies like **HDFC Bank**.

Quote by Morgan Housel:

"The stock market is a place where you can make money, but it also involves risk.

4. **Sensex**

The **Sensex** is the **BSE's** flagship index and is often considered a barometer of the Indian stock market. It includes 30 major, well-established companies that span across various sectors of the economy.

- **What is Sensex?**
  - Like the NIFTY 50, the Sensex provides a snapshot of the Indian economy. The index's value is a weighted average of the market prices of these 30 companies,

and it is used as a reference point for tracking market performance.

- **Example**:
  - **Tata Steel** and **ITC** are two companies listed in the Sensex. If you notice a drop in the Sensex, it could be due to a decline in stocks like Tata Steel or ITC, which are affected by both domestic and international factors like economic conditions, political events, or global demand for products.

Quote by Peter Lynch:

"Know what you own, and know why you own it."

The Role of Stock Indices

Both **NIFTY 50** and **Sensex** serve as benchmarks for the stock market's overall performance. Here's how they help you:

- **Track Market Trends**:
  - If the NIFTY or Sensex is rising, it generally signals a positive sentiment in the stock market, suggesting that many stocks are performing well. On the other hand, a decline might indicate market downturns or economic challenges.
- **Investment Decisions**:
  - These indices can help guide your investment decisions. For example, if you notice that the NIFTY is rising, you might consider investing in stocks of companies that are part of the index. Conversely,

if the Sensex is falling, it might be a good time to reevaluate your portfolio.

- **Market Sentiment**:
  - The movement of these indices helps investors gauge whether the market sentiment is bullish (optimistic) or bearish (pessimistic). A strong rise in the NIFTY or Sensex often indicates investor confidence in the economy, while a sharp decline might reflect concerns.

Quote by Robert Kiyosaki:

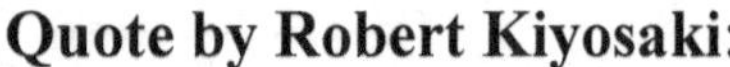

"The stock market is filled with individuals who know the price of everything, but the value of nothing."

Other Key Terms

Bull Market

A **bull market** refers to a phase where stock prices are rising consistently, driven by investor confidence, economic growth, or market optimism.

Example: During 2020-2021, the Indian stock market experienced a bull run as the economy recovered post-pandemic, with NIFTY 50 crossing the 18,000 mark for the first time.

Bear Market

A **bear market** occurs when stock prices fall by 20% or more from recent highs, often triggered by economic downturns or negative sentiment.

Example: In March 2020, due to the COVID-19 pandemic, the Sensex dropped from 40,000 to 25,000, marking a sharp bear market.

IPO (Initial Public Offering)

An **IPO** is when a private company offers its shares to the public for the first time. It's a way for companies to raise funds for expansion.

Example: When **Zomato** launched its IPO in 2021, investors could buy its shares at ₹76 per share. After listing, the shares saw significant trading activity, reflecting high demand.

Market Capitalization

Market capitalization refers to the total market value of a company's outstanding shares, calculated as: **Market Cap = Current Share Price × Total Number of Shares Outstanding**

Example: If **TCS** has 5 billion shares, each priced at ₹3,500, its market capitalization would be ₹17.5 trillion, classifying it as a large-cap company.

Role of Brokers and Demat Accounts

1. **Brokers**

   Brokers act as intermediaries who enable investors to buy and sell stocks. They provide trading platforms and charge fees or commissions for their services.

   Types of Brokers:

   1. **Full-Service Brokers:** Offer advisory services and research reports (e.g., **ICICI Direct**, **HDFC Securities**).

2. **Discount Brokers:** Focus on low-cost trading without advisory services (e.g., **Zerodha, Upstox**).

Example: If you decide to buy **HDFC Bank** shares, you can use platforms like Zerodha to place an order at a specified price. The broker executes the transaction on your behalf.

2. Demat Accounts

A **Demat Account** is an electronic storage system for holding stocks and securities. It eliminates the hassle of dealing with physical share certificates, making trading faster and more efficient.

Key Features:

- **Digital Transactions:** All shares are stored digitally, ensuring safety.
- **Ease of Use:** Buy and sell stocks with a click on platforms linked to your Demat Account.

Example: Let's say you purchase **5 shares of Infosys**. These shares will be credited to your Demat Account within two days (T+2 settlement cycle). You can then monitor them in your account via apps like Zerodha Kite or ICICI Direct.

How It All Works Together

When you want to invest in the stock market, you:

1. Open a **Demat and trading account** with a broker.
2. Deposit funds into your account.
3. Use your broker's platform to place buy/sell orders.
4. The broker executes the order on the NSE or BSE.
5. The purchased stocks are credited to your **Demat Account**.

Example Workflow:

- You log into your Zerodha account and decide to buy 10 shares of **HDFC Bank** at ₹1,650 each.
- Place a buy order through the trading platform.
- The order is executed on the NSE or BSE, and the shares are credited to your Demat Account.

Understanding Stock Valuation: Key to Smart Investing

Stock valuation helps investors determine whether a stock is fairly priced, undervalued, or overvalued compared to its intrinsic worth. Let's break this down with an explanation of the key metrics and practical examples:

Key Metrics

1. **P/E Ratio (Price-to-Earnings Ratio)**

   The **Price-to-Earnings (P/E) ratio** is one of the most commonly used tools to evaluate the valuation of a company's stock. It indicates how much investors are willing to pay for each rupee of earnings the company generates. The P/E ratio helps investors gauge whether a stock is overvalued or undervalued relative to its earnings and growth prospects.

   Formula for P/E Ratio:

   The P/E ratio is calculated using the following formula:

   P/E Ratio = Current Share Price / Earnings Per Share (EPS)

   Where:

   - **Current Share Price** is the market price of one share of the company's stock.

- **Earnings Per Share (EPS)** is the amount of profit the company generates for each share of stock outstanding.

Interpretation of P/E Ratio:

- **High P/E Ratio**: A high P/E ratio suggests that investors have high expectations for the company's future earnings growth. However, it could also mean that the stock is overvalued, especially if the company's earnings growth does not meet these expectations.
- **Low P/E Ratio**: A low P/E ratio might indicate that the stock is undervalued, or it could suggest that the company has lower growth potential. In some cases, a low P/E ratio might reflect market pessimism about the company's future performance.

The P/E ratio is useful for comparing companies within the same industry or sector. It can give you an idea of how much investors are willing to pay for earnings in relation to other companies in a similar space.

Example:

Let's take a look at two companies, **Company A** and **Company B**, to understand how the P/E ratio works:

- **Company A**:
  - **Current Share Price**: ₹500
  - **Earnings Per Share (EPS)**: ₹50
  - **P/E Ratio** = ₹500 / ₹50 = **10**
- **Company B**:
  - **Current Share Price**: ₹800

- **Earnings Per Share (EPS)**: ₹40
- **P/E Ratio** = ₹800 / ₹40 = **20**

Analysis:

- **Company A** has a **P/E ratio of 10**, which may suggest that the stock is relatively undervalued, assuming the company's fundamentals are strong. A lower P/E ratio can indicate that investors are not expecting significant growth, or the stock could simply be cheaper compared to other stocks in the market.
- **Company B** has a **P/E ratio of 20**, which is higher than Company A's. This indicates that investors have high expectations for the company's future earnings growth. However, a higher P/E ratio also means that investors are paying a premium for the stock. If the company fails to meet growth expectations, the stock could become overpriced.

Key Takeaways:

- **A high P/E ratio** generally indicates growth expectations, but it may also signal that the stock is overpriced if those expectations aren't met.
- **A low P/E ratio** might suggest that the stock is undervalued, but it could also mean that the company has low growth prospects or is facing challenges that investors are aware of.

Quote by Warren Buffett:

"Price is what you pay. Value is what you get."

2. **EPS (Earnings Per Share)**

   Earnings Per Share (EPS) is a key financial metric that helps assess a company's profitability on a per-share basis. It indicates how much profit a company is generating for each share of stock it has in circulation. EPS is widely used by investors to evaluate a company's performance and to compare it with other companies in the same industry.

   Formula for EPS:

   To calculate EPS, the formula is:

   EPS = Net Income / Outstanding Shares

   - **Net Income** refers to the company's total profit after accounting for all expenses, taxes, and other costs.
   - **Outstanding Shares** represents the total number of shares currently held by all shareholders, including institutional investors and insiders.

   By dividing the net income by the number of outstanding shares, you get the amount of profit attributable to each individual share.

   Interpretation of EPS:

   - **Higher EPS = Greater Profitability**: A higher EPS means that the company is more profitable per share. Investors tend to favor companies with higher EPS, as they indicate strong performance.
   - **Consistent EPS Growth**: If a company consistently shows growth in EPS over time, it is generally seen as a sign of good financial health and business

expansion. It suggests that the company is able to generate more profits as it grows.

- **Comparing Companies**: EPS is commonly used to compare the profitability of different companies. A company with a higher EPS is usually considered more profitable than one with a lower EPS, all else being equal.

Example:

Let's look at two companies, **Company C** and **Company D**, to better understand how EPS works:

- **Company C**:
  - **Net Income**: ₹10 crore
  - **Outstanding Shares**: 1 crore
  - **EPS** = ₹10 crore / 1 crore = ₹10 per share
- **Company D**:
  - **Net Income**: ₹20 crore
  - **Outstanding Shares**: 5 crore
  - **EPS** = ₹20 crore / 5 crore = ₹4 per share

Analysis:

- **Company C** has a higher EPS of ₹10 per share, meaning it is generating more profit for each share compared to **Company D**, which has an EPS of ₹4 per share.
- Despite having a higher total net income (₹20 crore vs ₹10 crore), **Company D** has more shares outstanding, which results in a lower EPS.
- **Investment Insight**: In this case, **Company C** might be more attractive to investors based on its higher

EPS, which indicates higher profitability on a per-share basis.

Additional Notes:

- **Diluted EPS**: Companies may issue convertible securities (like stock options or convertible bonds) that could increase the number of shares in circulation. In such cases, **diluted EPS** is calculated, which accounts for the potential increase in shares, thus providing a more conservative estimate of earnings per share.
- **EPS Growth**: It's important to track EPS growth over time. A company with consistently growing EPS is likely managing its operations well and expanding its business effectively.

Quote by Morgan Housel:

"The stock market is a device for transferring money from the impatient to the patient."

In summary, **Earnings Per Share (EPS)** is a vital indicator of a company's profitability and a valuable metric for comparing companies within the same industry. Understanding how to calculate and interpret EPS can help you make better-informed decisions as you evaluate potential investments.

3. **P/B Ratio (Price-to-Book Ratio)**

The **Price-to-Book (P/B) ratio** compares the market value of a stock with its book value (the net value of a company's assets).

Formula:

P/B Ratio = Current Share Price / Book Value Per Share

Interpretation:

- **Low P/B Ratio (< 1):**
  - Indicates undervaluation, making the stock attractive for value investors.
- **High P/B Ratio (> 1):**
  - Suggests the stock is trading above its book value, which could mean overvaluation.

Example:

- **Company E:**
  - Current share price = ₹200
  - Book value per share = ₹150
  - P/B Ratio = 200 / 150 = 1.33
- **Company F:**
  - Current share price = ₹120
  - Book value per share = ₹200
  - P/B Ratio = 120 / 200 = 0.6

Analysis:

- **Company E** has a P/B ratio of 1.33, indicating that the stock is trading above its book value, which may suggest it is overvalued.
- **Company F** has a P/B ratio of 0.6, meaning its market price is below its book value. This suggests that Company F might be undervalued, making it potentially attractive to value investors.

Valuation Insights

1. **Undervalued Stocks**

   An undervalued stock is trading below its intrinsic value, offering a **margin of safety** to investors. These stocks are attractive because they have the potential for higher returns when the market corrects itself.

   Example:

   A stock priced at ₹300 with strong fundamentals, an EPS of ₹20, and a P/E ratio of 15, while the industry average P/E is 20, might indicate it's undervalued.

   Benefits:

   - Provides opportunities for growth with lower downside risk.
   - Ideal for long-term investors.

2. **Overvalued Stocks**

   Overvalued stocks trade above their intrinsic value, making them risky, especially during market corrections. Investors might be paying a premium for growth that the company may not achieve.

   Example: A stock priced at ₹1,000 with an EPS of ₹25 and a P/E ratio of 40, compared to an industry average P/E of 20, might suggest it's overvalued.

   Risks:

   - Vulnerable to price drops during market downturns.
   - High reliance on speculative growth rather than fundamentals.

Practical Application

When evaluating stocks, use these metrics together rather than relying on one. For instance:

- A company with a **high P/E ratio** but consistently growing EPS might justify the premium price.
- A company with a **low P/B ratio** but declining EPS could signal underlying issues, even if it looks undervalued.

Types of Stocks: Understanding Investment Categories

Stocks can be categorized based on their characteristics, growth potential, and appeal to different investor profiles. Here's a deep dive into **growth stocks**, **dividend stocks**, and **penny stocks**, complete with examples and insights.

1. Growth Stocks

Definition: Growth stocks are shares of companies that are expected to grow their revenue and earnings at a faster rate than the overall market or their industry peers. These companies reinvest their profits to fuel expansion rather than paying dividends.

Key Features:

- **High Potential Returns:** Investors buy these stocks for capital appreciation, not dividends.
- **Innovative Sectors:** Often found in industries like technology, healthcare, and e-commerce.
- **Risk Profile:** Higher risk due to reliance on future growth, which may not always materialize.

Example:

- **Infosys:** In the 1990s, Infosys was considered a growth stock as it rapidly expanded during the IT boom. Investors who held shares during this period saw exponential returns.
- **Zomato:** As a tech-driven food delivery platform, Zomato represents a modern growth stock, reinvesting earnings to expand its market share.

Investor Profile:

- Suitable for younger, aggressive investors with a higher risk tolerance.
- Ideal for long-term investors who believe in the company's potential.

Risk Consideration: If the company fails to achieve expected growth, its stock price can plummet, leading to significant losses. For instance, startups in competitive sectors like ed-tech may face challenges scaling profitably.

2. Dividend Stocks

Definition: Dividend stocks are shares of well-established companies that regularly distribute a portion of their profits as dividends to shareholders. These stocks provide a steady income stream, making them appealing to conservative investors.

Key Features:

- **Regular Payouts:** Investors receive periodic income, regardless of stock price movement.

- **Stable Companies:** Typically found in mature industries with consistent earnings.
- **Lower Volatility:** Less volatile than growth or penny stocks, making them safer investments.

Example:

- **ITC:** A leading FMCG company known for its reliable dividend payouts, offering stability to investors.
- **NTPC:** A public-sector power company that consistently distributes dividends due to its predictable cash flows.

Investor Profile:

- Ideal for retirees or investors seeking a stable source of passive income.
- Suitable for risk-averse individuals prioritizing consistent returns over high growth.

Risk Consideration: Dividend stocks might underperform in terms of capital appreciation. For instance, utility companies with strong dividends may see limited growth due to market saturation.

3. **Penny Stocks**

Definition: Penny stocks are shares of small-cap companies priced at ₹10 or below per share. These stocks are highly speculative and often attract investors willing to take substantial risks for potentially high rewards.

Key Features:

- **Low Price:** Accessible to investors with limited capital.

- **High Risk and Volatility:** Prices can fluctuate dramatically within short periods.
- **Potential for High Returns:** If the company succeeds, penny stocks can deliver exponential gains.

Example:

- **Suzlon Energy:** Once a penny stock, it gained traction due to its renewable energy initiatives.
- **GTL Infrastructure:** A low-priced stock that experienced significant price swings based on market conditions.

Investor Profile:

- Suitable for speculative investors with a high-risk tolerance.
- Best for those who can closely monitor their portfolio and are willing to face potential losses.

Risk Consideration: Penny stocks are prone to market manipulation and lack transparency. Many small-cap companies fail to survive, leading to complete loss of investment. For example, shares of lesser-known startups may become worthless during financial crises.

Comparing Stock Types

Growth Stocks

- **Primary Benefit**: High capital appreciation
- **Risk Level**: High
- **Example Sectors**: Technology, e-commerce
- **Investor Profile**: Long-term growth-focused investors

Growth stocks are typically from companies that show strong growth potential, especially in sectors like technology or e-commerce. These stocks carry a higher risk but offer the potential for significant returns over the long term. They are ideal for investors who are focused on capital appreciation and are willing to accept market volatility for higher potential rewards.

Dividend Stocks

- **Primary Benefit**: Regular income
- **Risk Level**: Low to moderate
- **Example Sectors**: FMCG, utilities
- **Investor Profile**: Conservative, income-focused investors

Dividend stocks are typically from well-established companies that pay regular dividends. These stocks are usually less risky than growth stocks and are favored by conservative investors looking for regular income. They are common in sectors like FMCG (Fast-Moving Consumer Goods) and utilities, where steady cash flow is a hallmark of the business model.

Penny Stocks

- **Primary Benefit**: Low-cost, high-reward potential
- **Risk Level**: Very high
- **Example Sectors**: Small-cap industries
- **Investor Profile**: Speculative, high-risk takers

Penny stocks are low-priced stocks, often from small-cap companies, that can offer huge rewards if the company performs well. However, they are highly speculative and carry very high risk. These stocks are often highly volatile and are suited for investors willing to take on substantial risk for the chance of large returns.

Conclusion

Each type of stock serves a different purpose within a portfolio.

- **Growth stocks** are ideal for building wealth over time but carry higher risks.
- **Dividend stocks** provide stability and regular income, making them perfect for conservative investors.
- **Penny stocks** offer the allure of massive gains but come with significant volatility and risk.

A balanced portfolio often includes a mix of these stock types to align with an investor's goals, risk tolerance, and time horizon.

How to Pick the Right Stock: A Strategic Approach

Investing in stocks requires a careful evaluation of various factors to ensure that the company is poised for growth, has sound financials, and operates in a promising industry. Here are key indicators and strategies for choosing the right stock.

Key Indicators for Picking the Right Stock

1. **Financial Health**

   A company's financial health is a key factor in determining its ability to generate profit and withstand market volatility. Here's how you can assess a company's financial stability:

- **Debt-to-Equity Ratio:**

  This metric compares the company's total debt to shareholders' equity, helping assess financial leverage and risk. A high ratio indicates the company is heavily reliant on debt, which could be risky in times of economic downturn. A lower ratio suggests better financial stability.

  Example:

  - Company A has a debt-to-equity ratio of 0.2, indicating it is not overly reliant on debt.
  - Company B has a ratio of 1.5, suggesting it is highly leveraged, which may be risky.

- **Revenue Growth:**

  A consistent increase in revenue signals a growing and expanding company. Analyze the revenue trend over the past 3-5 years to understand the business trajectory.

  Example:

  - Company X has grown its revenue by 10% year-over-year for the last 5 years, indicating healthy expansion.

- **Profitability Metrics:**
  - **Gross Profit Margin:** Measures the efficiency of the company's core business activities. Higher margins are better.
  - **Net Profit Margin:** Indicates overall profitability after all expenses.

- **Example:**
- Company Y has a gross profit margin of 50%, meaning for every ₹100 in sales, it keeps ₹50 as gross profit, which is healthy for a manufacturing business.
- Company Z has a net profit margin of 5%, indicating lower overall profitability.

By reviewing these financial metrics, investors can assess whether a company is financially sound and capable of managing its growth.

2. **Management Quality**

The leadership of a company plays a crucial role in its long-term success. Investors should assess the quality of the management team based on the following factors:

- **Vision and Strategy:** Does the leadership have a clear and achievable vision for the company's future? Are they transparent about their plans and goals?

Example:

- **Mukesh Ambani** of Reliance Industries has a clear strategy of diversifying into telecom and retail, which has significantly expanded the company's value in recent years.

- **Ethical Standing:**
- Are the leaders of the company involved in any ethical or legal issues? A company with transparent, ethical management tends to perform better in the long run.

Example:

- ○ **Tata Group** is known for its ethical approach to business, contributing to long-term shareholder trust and growth.

- ➤ **Experience and Track Record:**

  Evaluate the leadership's experience and historical performance. A strong management team with a proven track record in driving business success is vital for sustained growth.

Example:

- ○ **Indra Nooyi**, former CEO of PepsiCo, led the company through significant global expansion, showcasing the importance of experienced leadership.

3. **Industry Trends**

Understanding the macroeconomic landscape and industry-specific trends can help you identify sectors that are expected to grow in the future.

- ➤ **Macroeconomic Indicators:**

  Study factors such as GDP growth, inflation rates, and interest rates, as these affect market performance.

  Example:

- ○ The **renewable energy sector** is expected to grow as governments push for clean energy initiatives, making companies in this sector attractive for long-term investments.

- **Sector-specific Growth:**

  Some sectors, like **IT, renewable energy, pharmaceuticals**, and **fintech**, are poised for significant growth. Research trends in these industries and the companies that are leading the charge.

Example:

- **Pharmaceuticals** saw a huge boost during the COVID-19 pandemic, with companies like **Cipla** and **Dr. Reddy's Laboratories** benefiting from increased demand for vaccines and medicines.

By evaluating industry trends, you can align your investments with sectors that are expected to thrive, improving the potential for growth.

Stock Market Regulations: Safeguarding Investors

In India, the stock market is heavily regulated to ensure fairness, transparency, and protection for investors. The Securities and Exchange Board of India (SEBI) plays a critical role in overseeing **the operations of the stock market.**

SEBI's Role

Securities and Exchange Board of India (SEBI) is the regulatory authority that oversees the functioning of the stock market in India. It is responsible for maintaining market integrity and protecting investor interests by:

- **Regulating Market Operations:** SEBI ensures that market participants, including brokers and exchanges, operate in a fair and transparent manner. This includes preventing market manipulation, insider trading, and other unethical practices.

- **Enforcing Disclosure Norms:** Companies are required to disclose their financial results, shareholding patterns, and material developments regularly. This ensures investors have access to timely and accurate information to make informed decisions.

  Example: Companies listed on the **NSE** or **BSE** must adhere to SEBI's stringent disclosure requirements to maintain investor confidence.

- **Investor Protection:** SEBI also works to protect investors by promoting awareness and implementing investor-friendly policies like the Investor Protection Fund, which compensates investors in case of broker defaults or fraud.

Transparency and Scam Prevention

To avoid falling victim to scams and fraudulent schemes, investors should focus on the following guidelines:

- **Avoid Dubious Schemes:** Be cautious of investment opportunities that promise extraordinarily high returns in a short period. These are often indicators of fraud or pyramid schemes.

Example:

- Companies promising returns of 30-40% annually with no clear business model should raise red flags.

- **Stick to SEBI-Compliant Investments:** Invest in companies listed on SEBI-compliant exchanges (such as the **NSE** and **BSE**), which follow strict regulations for transparency and disclosures.

Example:

- Investing in well-known companies like **Reliance**, **HDFC**, or **Infosys** that have a strong, verifiable track record and adhere to SEBI regulations.

By staying informed and adhering to regulatory guidelines, investors can protect themselves from scams and make safer, more informed investment choices.

Creating a Stock Portfolio: Strategies for Risk Management and Goal Alignment

Building a well-structured stock portfolio is crucial to managing risk while achieving long-term financial goals. A diversified portfolio that balances different types of investments can help minimize potential losses and optimize returns. Let's explore key concepts in creating a strong stock portfolio, including **diversification** and **balancing goals**.

Diversification: The Key to Reducing Risk

Diversification involves spreading your investments across different **sectors** and **asset classes** to reduce the impact of any one underperforming investment on the overall portfolio. By not putting all your eggs in one basket, you can protect yourself from market volatility and mitigate risks associated with a single asset or sector.

1. **Sector Diversification**

   Investing across various sectors ensures that the performance of one sector doesn't disproportionately affect your overall portfolio. For example:

   - **IT Sector**: Technology stocks like **Infosys**, **TCS**, and **Wipro** tend to grow rapidly due to the increasing demand for digital services.
   - **Banking Sector**: Stocks like **HDFC Bank** and **ICICI Bank** provide stability and consistent returns through dividends and interest income.
   - **Healthcare Sector**: Companies like **Dr. Reddy's Laboratories** or **Apollo Hospitals** thrive in times of health crises and continue to grow with the expanding healthcare needs.

   Example of Sector Allocation:

   If the economy goes through a rough patch, the banking sector may remain stable, while the IT sector might see more fluctuations. A diversified portfolio can balance the risk from one sector with the stability from others.

2. **Asset Class Diversification**

   Along with sector diversification, it's also crucial to diversify your portfolio across different asset classes, such as:

   - **Equity** (stocks)
   - **Debt** (bonds, fixed-income instruments)
   - **Commodities** (gold, real estate)
   - **Cash equivalents** (money market funds, short-term deposits)

Example: A well-diversified portfolio might look like:

- **50% in Blue-Chip Stocks**: These are large, established companies with a proven track record of stable earnings and dividends (e.g., **Reliance, HDFC Bank**).
- **30% in Mid-Cap Stocks**: These are growing companies with higher growth potential but also higher risk. Examples include companies like **Lupin Pharmaceuticals** or **Godrej Consumer Products**.
- **20% in Fixed-Income Assets**: Bonds, government securities, or fixed deposits that provide regular income with lower risk.

Why Diversify?

- **Risk Reduction**: Not all asset classes or sectors move in the same direction. If the equity market falls, your bonds or gold holdings may still perform well, protecting your portfolio from significant losses.
- **Higher Returns**: A diversified portfolio can enhance returns by capturing opportunities across multiple asset classes that are in different market cycles.

Balancing Goals: Aligning Short-Term and Long-Term Investments

An effective stock portfolio balances both **short-term** and **long-term** financial goals, allowing you to meet immediate needs while ensuring long-term wealth creation.

1. **Short-Term Goals: Tactical Investments**

   Short-term goals are typically those you aim to achieve in the next 1 to 3 years, such as funding a vacation, purchasing a car, or creating an emergency fund. Investments for these goals need to prioritize **liquidity** and **capital preservation**.

   ➢ **Tactical Approach**:

   ○ Invest in assets that are less volatile and offer quicker returns, such as **blue-chip stocks**, **debt funds**, or **short-term bonds**.

   ○ Avoid high-risk assets like penny stocks, which can fluctuate dramatically in the short term.

   Example:

   ➢ If you plan to buy a car in the next 1-2 years, you might allocate 70% of your short-term portfolio to low-risk debt instruments (such as fixed deposits) and 30% in blue-chip stocks that offer stability.

2. **Long-Term Goals: Wealth Creation and Compounding**

   Long-term goals are those you aim to achieve in 5 years or more, such as building a retirement corpus or funding your child's education. The focus here should be on **wealth creation** and taking advantage of the power of **compounding**.

   ➢ **Growth-Oriented Approach**:

   ○ Invest in higher-risk, higher-reward assets like **equity** (growth stocks, mid-cap stocks, index funds) and **mutual funds** that can generate significant returns over time.

- Let your investments compound over time by reinvesting dividends and allowing the value of your investments to appreciate.

Example:

- For long-term goals like retirement, allocate the majority of your portfolio (e.g., 70-80%) to equities (growth stocks, diversified index funds) to leverage compounding. The remaining portion can be invested in bonds or debt funds to reduce volatility.

Creating a Balanced Portfolio: Example Allocations

Here are three different example portfolios based on risk tolerance and financial goals:

1. **Conservative Portfolio (Low Risk)**
   - **40% in Debt Instruments** (bonds, fixed deposits)
   - **30% in Blue-Chip Stocks** (e.g., **Reliance**, **Tata Consultancy Services**)
   - **20% in Gold/Commodities** (a safe haven asset)
   - **10% in Cash Equivalents** (money market funds, savings accounts)

   This portfolio focuses on capital preservation with minimal risk, suited for investors seeking steady income and low exposure to market volatility.

2. **Balanced Portfolio (Moderate Risk)**
   - **30% in Debt Instruments**
   - **40% in Blue-Chip and Mid-Cap Stocks**
   - **20% in Equity Mutual Funds/Index Funds**
   - **10% in Commodities or Gold**

This portfolio aims for balanced growth, with an equal emphasis on stable income and moderate growth, making it ideal for individuals with a medium-term investment horizon (5-10 years).

3. **Growth-Oriented Portfolio (High Risk)**
   - **10% in Debt Instruments**
   - **50% in Growth Stocks** (e.g., technology, healthcare, fintech)
   - **30% in Mid-Cap Stocks**
   - **10% in Commodities or Gold**

   This portfolio is suitable for long-term investors with a high-risk tolerance who seek high growth, potentially sacrificing short-term stability for long-term wealth creation.

Managing Market Volatility: Strategies for Staying Calm and Building Resilience

Market volatility is an inevitable part of investing, especially in the stock market, where prices can fluctuate drastically due to factors like economic conditions, geopolitical events, or market sentiment. While it's tempting to react impulsively to market dips, a disciplined and strategic approach can help you manage volatility effectively. Here are key strategies for **staying calm** and **building resilience** during turbulent times.

Staying Calm: Focused Investing Amidst Volatility

1. **Dollar-Cost Averaging (DCA)**

   Dollar-cost averaging is a strategy where you invest a fixed amount of money at regular intervals (e.g., monthly or quarterly) regardless of the market price at the time. This approach helps reduce the impact of market volatility and smoothens out the cost of buying assets over time.

- **How It Works:**
  - You invest a fixed amount, say ₹5,000, every month into an equity mutual fund or stocks.
  - When the market is down, you buy more units for the same amount, and when the market is up, you buy fewer units.
  - Over time, this lowers the average cost per unit, reducing the risk of investing a lump sum at a market peak.
- **Example:** Imagine you plan to invest ₹60,000 over a year. Instead of investing ₹60,000 at once, you invest ₹5,000 each month.
  - In **Month 1**, the stock price is ₹100, so you purchase 50 units.
  - In **Month 2**, the stock price falls to ₹80, so you purchase 62.5 units.
  - In **Month 3**, the stock price rises to ₹120, so you purchase 41.67 units.
  - Over the year, you have purchased stocks at different price points, reducing the risk of buying all the shares when the market was at a peak.

Benefits of Dollar-Cost Averaging:

- **Reduces the impact of market fluctuations**: By spreading out your investments, you don't risk buying at the highest price point.

- **Removes emotional decision-making**: Regular, automated investing prevents you from trying to time the market, which is often difficult and leads to poor investment decisions.

2. **Long-Term Investing: The Power of Patience**

A long-term investment strategy focuses on holding investments for several years, often decades, to ride out market fluctuations and take advantage of compound growth. This approach shifts the focus from short-term volatility to long-term financial goals.

- **How Long-Term Investing Helps:**
  - Stock markets tend to show significant growth over long periods, despite short-term dips. By staying invested through downturns, investors can benefit from the overall upward trajectory of the market.
  - Historically, the Indian stock market, as represented by indices like the **Sensex** or **NIFTY**, has shown consistent growth over 5-10 year periods, even though it has experienced multiple short-term crashes.
- **Example:**
  - If you had invested ₹1,00,000 in **NIFTY 50** 10 years ago, your investment would have grown considerably, even though the market experienced occasional declines.
  - If you had sold during a market dip, you would have missed out on the recovery and growth that followed.

Benefits of Long-Term Investing:

- **Compounding**: The longer you stay invested, the more your money works for you through compounding.
- **Reduced Impact of Volatility**: By not reacting to short-term dips, you allow your investments to recover and grow over time.
- **Focus on Financial Goals**: Long-term investors keep their eye on their financial goals (retirement, wealth accumulation) rather than getting distracted by short-term market fluctuations.

Building Resilience: Strengthening Your Financial Foundation

1. Develop an Emergency Fund

Having an emergency fund is one of the most crucial steps in building resilience against financial stress during market downturns. An emergency fund acts as a financial cushion, allowing you to manage unforeseen expenses without needing to liquidate investments during a market slump.

- **How Much to Save**:
  - Ideally, your emergency fund should cover **3-6 months of living expenses** to ensure you can sustain yourself without needing to dip into your investments. This is especially important during market downturns when you might not want to sell investments at a loss.

- **Where to Keep Your Emergency Fund**:
  - The fund should be kept in a **liquid, low-risk** instrument such as a **high-interest savings account** or **fixed deposit**. This ensures that you can access the money quickly when needed without sacrificing returns from more volatile investments.
- **Example**: If your monthly living expenses are ₹50,000, aim to have an emergency fund of ₹2,50,000–₹3,00,000. If the market is experiencing a downturn, you can rely on your emergency fund for expenses without the need to sell investments at a loss.

2. **Avoid Impulsive Decisions Based on Market Sentiment**

   It's common for investors to make decisions based on emotions, especially during periods of market volatility. The fear of losing money during a market crash or the greed to capitalize on a short-term rally can lead to poor investment decisions. To manage this:

   - **Stick to Your Strategy**: Revisit your investment strategy periodically to ensure it aligns with your long-term goals. If you're using a dollar-cost averaging strategy, continue investing regularly, regardless of market conditions.
   - **Review Fundamentals, Not Headlines**: During market downturns, it's crucial to focus on the **fundamentals** of your investments rather than reacting to market news or sentiment. If the company's financial health, growth prospects, and management remain solid, there may be no reason to sell.

3

The Indian Investor's Guide to Financial Independence

The Basics of Financial Independence (FI)

Financial Independence (FI) refers to a state where your investments and passive income cover your living expenses, liberating you from the need to work for a paycheck. It's about having control over your time, pursuing passions, and focusing on what matters most without financial constraints. In India, this concept is gaining traction due to rising awareness about quality of life, financial literacy, and the desire for work-life balance.

1. **What is Financial Independence?**

   Financial Independence is the ability to live comfortably without having to depend on a regular job or active income. Instead, your wealth—generated through savings, investments, and passive income streams—supports your lifestyle. Achieving financial independence allows you to make life decisions without the pressure of earning money to meet your basic needs.

Key Features of Financial Independence:

- **No Need for Active Income**: Once you achieve financial independence, your income comes from your investments, savings, or other sources like dividends, interest, or rental income. This reduces the need to work for money.
- **Freedom to Choose**: Financial independence gives you the freedom to pursue your passions, hobbies, or new ventures without being constrained by financial concerns.
- **Long-Term Security**: It provides a safety net, ensuring you can maintain your lifestyle, even during economic downturns or job loss.

Example of Achieving Financial Independence:

- Let's say you are a **technology professional earning ₹1,00,000 per month**. You decide to save **₹40,000 each month** and invest this amount in **equity mutual funds**. Assuming an average annual return of **12%**, after **20 years**, your total savings could grow to **₹2.4 crore**.
- By using a **Systematic Withdrawal Plan**, this ₹2.4 crore corpus could generate about **₹80,000 per month**, which would replace your active income, enabling you to live off your investments and achieve financial independence.

"Financial freedom is available to those who learn about it and work for it."

–**Robert Kiyosaki**

2. **Why is Financial Independence Becoming Popular in India?**

Several factors are driving the increasing interest in financial independence in India. These include rising awareness about personal finance, economic shifts, changing attitudes towards work and money, and the influence of global movements.

Increased Awareness

- **Access to Financial Education**: Platforms like **YouTube**, personal finance blogs, and books have made financial education accessible to millions of people in India. More individuals now understand the importance of managing their money wisely and planning for their future. As a result, financial independence is becoming a realistic goal for many.

Economic Shifts

- **Impact of the COVID-19 Pandemic**: The **COVID-19 pandemic** highlighted the importance of having a financial safety net. Many people lost their jobs or saw their incomes reduced during the crisis. This made many realize how vulnerable they were without an emergency fund or passive income streams. The pandemic acted as a wake-up call for many people to take control of their finances and pursue financial independence.
- **Job Insecurity**: In today's rapidly changing job market, many sectors, such as hospitality, aviation, and retail, are facing challenges. This has led to an

increased desire for financial security, with more people exploring ways to create alternative income sources, such as investing in the stock market, mutual funds, or real estate.

Changing Lifestyles

- **Millennials and Generation Z**: Younger generations are less focused on accumulating material possessions and more interested in having flexible lifestyles, pursuing experiences, and maintaining a work-life balance. This shift in mindset has made financial independence appealing, as it offers the freedom to live life on their own terms, without being tied to a conventional job.
- **Desire for Career Flexibility**: With the rise of **freelancing**, **remote work**, and **side hustles**, many people now prefer to build their financial independence through multiple income streams. Financial independence allows them to achieve this flexibility, without the need for a traditional 9-to-5 job.

Global Movements: The Financial Independence, Retire Early Movement

- **Global Influence of Financial Independence, Retire Early**: The **Financial Independence, Retire Early** movement, which started in the Western world, has gained significant traction in India. The idea of achieving financial independence and retiring early is becoming increasingly popular among young professionals. By aggressively saving and investing, the goal is to build a large enough corpus that generates passive income, allowing you to retire much earlier than the typical retirement age.

- **Inspiration from Global Stories**: Many successful financial independence stories from around the world are being shared through blogs, books, and YouTube channels. These stories, along with a growing number of Indian blogs and social media accounts, have inspired more people in India to explore financial independence as a viable goal.

Example: *In India, cities like Bengaluru, Mumbai, and Delhi are seeing a growing number of people embracing the Financial Independence, Retire Early movement. The combination of high-paying jobs, lower costs of living compared to Western cities, and greater access to investment opportunities is making early retirement a more achievable goal.*

Quote by Tim Ferriss:

"Money is a tool. It's a means to an end, not the end itself."

The Concept of Early Retirement and Financial Freedom

The idea of **early retirement** and **financial freedom** has become increasingly popular, especially among younger individuals looking for more control over their lives and finances. While many people dream of retirement, the concept of retiring early—often referred to as **Early Retirement** or **Financial Independence, Retire Early (FIRE)**—has grown in appeal as people seek to free themselves from the traditional 9-to-5 grind. In this section, we'll break down what early retirement and financial freedom truly mean and explore how these goals are achievable through strategic financial planning and disciplined investing.

1. **Early Retirement Explained**

   Early retirement doesn't necessarily mean quitting work altogether. Instead, it's about **achieving financial independence** to the point where you no longer have to work for money. It gives you the freedom to choose work that aligns with your passions and interests rather than doing something solely out of financial necessity.

   Key Points:

   - **Work Based on Passion, Not Obligation**: Early retirees often transition to work that excites them, like freelancing, consulting, or even starting a business. This kind of work gives them fulfillment without the pressure of earning a paycheck to meet basic needs.
   - **Achieving Early Retirement**: Early retirement is typically achieved through disciplined saving and investing. By building up a significant **investment portfolio**, individuals can generate passive income that supports their lifestyle without the need for regular employment.

Quote by Brian Tracy:

"The key to financial freedom and great wealth is a person's ability to convert earned income into passive income or portfolio income."

2. Financial Freedom Defined

While **early retirement** focuses on leaving full-time work behind, **financial freedom** is a broader concept that encompasses a variety of financial goals, including debt elimination, sustainable living, and the ability to make choices without constantly worrying about money. It's not just about retiring early; it's about reaching a point where you no longer have to stress over financial decisions or how to meet your basic needs.

Key Points:

- **Debt-Free Living**: Achieving financial freedom often starts with paying off high-interest debt, such as personal loans, credit card balances, or car loans. Reducing or eliminating debt frees up more money that can be saved or invested.
- **Sustainable Living**: Living below your means and prioritizing long-term financial goals over short-term gratification helps create a stable foundation for financial freedom. It's about building good financial habits that will pay off in the long run.
- **Pursuing Your Goals**: Financial freedom gives you the liberty to focus on your passions, whether that's starting a business, pursuing a hobby, or traveling,

without worrying about how to pay for it. It offers **autonomy** over your financial future.

Quote by Napoleon Hill:

"What the mind of man can conceive and believe, it can achieve."

How to Achieve Financial Independence and Early Retirement

While the specific paths to early retirement and financial freedom will vary depending on individual circumstances, here are some **key strategies** to work towards these goals:

- **Save Aggressively**: The more you save, the sooner you can retire. Many early retirees aim to save at least **50% of their income**. The higher your savings rate, the faster you'll reach your goal.
- **Invest Wisely**: Focus on building a **diverse investment portfolio** that includes stocks, bonds, mutual funds, real estate, and other assets. Consistently investing in **equity mutual funds** or **index funds** can provide you with strong returns over time.
- **Cut Unnecessary Expenses**: Living below your means is crucial to financial independence. Track your spending and eliminate unnecessary expenses. This doesn't mean cutting out all enjoyment, but it's about being mindful of where your money goes.
- **Create Passive Income**: Develop streams of income that don't require your active involvement. This could

include rental income, dividends from investments, or even income from a small business.

- **Plan for the Long Term**: Financial independence is a long-term goal that requires patience. Set clear financial goals and revisit them regularly to stay on track.

Quote by Shiv Khera:

"Success is not the key to happiness. Happiness is the key to success. If you love what you are doing, you will be successful."

Steps to Achieving Financial Independence in India

Achieving **financial independence (FI)** in India requires a disciplined approach to savings, investing, and managing expenses. The key is to build wealth over time through strategic financial planning and creating a solid foundation. Below are the essential steps to help you work towards financial independence and gain the freedom to live life on your terms.

1. **Set a Clear Goal:**

   Setting a clear financial goal is the first step toward achieving financial independence. You need to calculate how much money you will need to support your lifestyle once you no longer rely on an active income.

   How to Calculate Your FI Corpus:

   - Estimate your **monthly expenses**. This includes all regular living costs—rent, groceries, bills, transportation, entertainment, etc.

- Multiply your monthly expenses by **300**. This figure is based on the **4% withdrawal rule**, which suggests that if you withdraw 4% of your invested corpus annually, it will last you for at least 30 years.

Example:

- Let's say your **monthly expenses** are ₹50,000.
- Multiply ₹50,000 by **300**, which gives you a required corpus of **₹1.5 crore** to be financially independent.
- This means that if you have ₹1.5 crore invested in assets that give you an annual return, you could safely withdraw 4% (₹6,00,000 per year, or ₹50,000 per month) to cover your expenses without depleting your savings.

Quote by Robert Kiyosaki:

"It's not about how much money you make. It's about how much money you keep, how hard it works for you, and how many generations you keep it for."

2. **Build an Emergency Fund:**

   Before you start aggressively investing for long-term wealth, it's important to have a **financial safety net**—an **emergency fund**. This fund ensures that you're prepared for unexpected events like medical emergencies, job loss, or urgent repairs.

How to Build an Emergency Fund:

- **Target 6-12 months of expenses**. This gives you enough liquidity to cover unforeseen costs without having to dip into your investments.
- **Use liquid instruments**: You should park this fund in low-risk, easily accessible assets like a **savings account**, **liquid mutual funds**, or **short-term fixed deposits**.

Quote by Morgan Housel:

"The only thing that is guaranteed is uncertainty. The best way to prepare for the unknown is to save and invest."

3. **Invest Wisely:**

The core of financial independence lies in **building wealth through investments**. While saving alone will not generate significant wealth, strategic investing can help your money grow.

Key Investment Strategies:

- **Systematic Investment Plans (SIPs) in equity mutual funds**: SIPs allow you to invest a fixed amount regularly in **equity mutual funds**, which tend to offer higher returns over the long term. SIPs also help you benefit from **rupee cost averaging**, minimizing the impact of market volatility.
- **Diversify across asset classes**: Don't put all your money in one basket. Build a **diversified portfolio** by investing in different asset classes like:

- ○ **Public Provident Fund (PPF)**: A safe, government-backed long-term investment with tax benefits.
- ○ **National Pension Scheme (NPS)**: A retirement-focused investment that also provides tax benefits.
- ○ **Gold**: A traditional asset class that can hedge against inflation.

- **Real Estate Investment Trusts (REITs)**: These are a way to invest in real estate without the need to own property. REITs provide **regular dividend income** and can offer long-term capital appreciation.

Example:

- If you invest ₹15,000 per month in **equity mutual funds** for 20 years, assuming a **12% annual return**, you could accumulate a corpus of **₹1 crore**. Over time, the power of compounding will allow your money to grow substantially.

Quote by Brian Tracy:

"The greatest investment you can make is in yourself. You have to get educated. You have to learn how to invest. You have to learn how to become financially independent."

4. **Eliminate Debt:**

Debt, especially **high-interest debt**, can be a significant obstacle to achieving financial independence. Paying off debt should be a priority, as the money spent on interest could otherwise be invested to build wealth.

How to Eliminate Debt:

- Focus on paying off **high-interest debt** first, such as credit card debt or personal loans. These types of loans have high interest rates, which make them expensive to carry.
- Once high-interest debts are cleared, focus on clearing other loans, such as car loans, home loans, or education loans.

Example:

- If you are paying **₹50,000 per year** on a **credit card loan**, instead of continuing to pay this amount, use that money to **prepay the loan**. Once the debt is cleared, you can redirect the money you were using to pay off the loan into **investments**.
- Clearing debts allows you to free up more money for saving and investing, accelerating your path to financial independence.

Quote by Napoleon Hill:

"The way to wealth is through the use of money, but the way to financial independence is through the elimination of debt."

5. **Create Passive Income Streams:**

To achieve financial independence, you need to generate income that doesn't require active effort. This is where **passive income** comes in—earning money without working for it directly.

How to Build Passive Income:

- **Rent Out Property**: If you own real estate, renting out property can provide a steady stream of income.
- **Invest in Dividend-Paying Stocks**: Many companies pay regular dividends to their shareholders. By investing in **dividend-paying stocks**, you can create a passive income stream.
- **Start a Side Hustle**: If you have a passion or a skill, consider turning it into a source of income. For example, starting an online business, freelance work, or selling products or services can help generate additional income.

Example:

- Suppose you own a **₹50 lakh apartment** and rent it out for **₹15,000 per month**. This rental income can cover a portion of your living expenses, giving you more flexibility in your financial planning.
- Over time, you can use this rental income to reinvest and build wealth.

Quote by Shiv Khera:

"You don't have to be great to start, but you have to start to be great."

Indian Challenges and Solutions

1. **High Inflation:** Indian inflation averages 5-6%, eroding purchasing power.

   Solution: Focus on equity investments, which historically provide 10-12% returns.

2. **Family Responsibilities:** Joint families often mean higher expenses.
   Solution: Invest in flexible instruments like ELSS or ULIPs for tax efficiency and growth.
3. **Taxes on Investments:** Taxes can reduce returns significantly.
   Solution: Maximize deductions under Section 80C, invest in tax-free bonds, and opt for long-term equity investments to minimize taxes.

How Much Do You Need to Retire Early?

Early retirement requires careful planning to determine the *retirement number*—the amount of money you need to sustain your lifestyle without active income. This is primarily done using the **4% rule** while accounting for living expenses and inflation.

1. **Calculating Your Retirement Number Using the 4% Rule**

   The **4% rule** is a widely accepted guideline that states you can withdraw 4% of your retirement corpus annually without running out of money for at least 30 years.

   Steps to Calculate Your Retirement Number:

   1. Estimate your annual expenses.
   2. Multiply this amount by 25 (inverse of 4%) to calculate the corpus needed.

   Example 1: Single Individual (Urban)

   - Monthly expenses: ₹50,000 (₹6,00,000 annually)
   - Retirement corpus = ₹6,00,000 × 25 = ₹1.5 crore.

- At a 4% withdrawal rate, ₹1.5 crore generates ₹6,00,000 annually or ₹50,000/month.

Example 2: Family of Four (Suburban)

- Monthly expenses: ₹75,000 (₹9,00,000 annually)
- Retirement corpus = ₹9,00,000 × 25 = ₹2.25 crore.
- This corpus ensures ₹75,000/month for living expenses.

2. **Estimating Living Expenses and Future Inflation**

   Inflation erodes the purchasing power of money, so it's crucial to adjust your retirement number to account for future costs. In India, inflation has historically averaged 5-6% annually.

Steps to Estimate Future Expenses:

Estimating your future expenses is an important part of retirement planning, as it helps you determine how much money you'll need to maintain your lifestyle when you stop working. One of the key factors to account for is **inflation**, which erodes the purchasing power of your money over time. Below are the steps to estimate your future expenses accurately.

Step 1: Calculate Current Monthly Expenses

Begin by listing all your current monthly expenses. This should include:

- **Essentials**: Rent, utilities, groceries, transportation, healthcare, etc.
- **Discretionary Expenses**: Entertainment, dining out, travel, etc.

- **Savings and Investments**: Amount set aside for retirement, emergency fund, or other financial goals.

For example, let's assume your current monthly expenses are ₹50,000.

Step 2: Use the Future Value Formula to Project Costs

Next, you need to account for inflation to estimate how much those expenses will increase in the future. The formula for estimating future expenses is:

Future Value = Present Value × (1 + Inflation Rate) ^ Years

Where:

- **Present Value** is your current monthly expense.
- **Inflation Rate** is the expected annual inflation rate (expressed as a decimal).
- **Years** is the number of years into the future you want to project.

The formula helps you determine how your expenses will grow as prices increase over time.

Example: Future Expenses Calculation

Let's take the following assumptions:

- **Current Monthly Expenses**: ₹50,000
- **Inflation Rate**: 6% (0.06)
- **Time Period**: 20 years (for retirement)

To estimate your future monthly expenses:

Future Monthly Expenses = ₹50,000 × (1 + 0.06) ^ 20

Future Monthly Expenses = ₹50,000 × (1.06) ^ 20

Future Monthly Expenses ≈ ₹1,60,000

So, in 20 years, your monthly expenses could rise to ₹1,60,000 due to inflation.

Step 3: Calculate Adjusted Corpus Using the 4% Rule

Once you have your estimated future monthly expenses, you can use the **4% rule** to estimate how much you need to save for retirement. The 4% rule states that you can safely withdraw 4% of your total retirement corpus each year to cover your expenses, without depleting your savings.

To calculate your retirement corpus:

1. **Annual Expenses** = Future Monthly Expenses × 12
   Annual Expenses = ₹1,60,000 × 12 = ₹19,20,000
2. **Retirement Corpus** = Annual Expenses × 25 (based on the 4% rule)

Retirement Corpus = ₹19,20,000 × 25 = ₹4.8 crore

This means that you would need a retirement corpus of ₹4.8 crore to comfortably support an annual expenditure of ₹19.2 lakh, allowing you to withdraw 4% each year to meet your future expenses.

3. **Key Considerations for Accurate Planning**
   1. **Healthcare Costs:**
      Medical expenses tend to rise significantly in later years. Include provisions for health insurance or create a dedicated healthcare fund.

   Example:
   - A ₹25 lakh health fund, growing at 8% annually, will cover future costs without depleting your main corpus.

   2. **Lifestyle Choices:** Your retirement expenses will vary depending on your lifestyle goals:

- *Basic Retirement:* Focus on essential expenses like housing and food.
- *Comfortable Retirement:* Include travel, hobbies, and occasional luxuries.

3. **Multiple Income Streams:** Supplement your corpus with income from:
   - Dividends
   - Rental income
   - Part-time consulting or freelancing.
4. **Emergency Provisions:** Build a separate fund for unforeseen events like medical emergencies, repairs, or economic downturns.

Real-Life Example: Achieving the Right Corpus

Case Study: Rahul's Early Retirement Plan

Rahul, a 30-year-old software engineer from Pune, plans to retire at 45, which gives him 15 years to prepare financially. Let's break down his plan and calculate how much he needs to save to achieve his goal of financial independence.

Step 1: Calculate Future Expenses in 15 Years

- **Current Monthly Expenses**: ₹70,000
- **Estimated Inflation Rate**: 6% per year
- **Time Period**: 15 years

To estimate Rahul's future expenses, we need to account for the impact of inflation on his current expenses. The formula to calculate future expenses is:

Future Expenses = Current Expenses × (1 + Inflation Rate) ^ Years

Here's how it works:

- **Current Expenses**: ₹70,000
- **Inflation Rate**: 6% (written as 0.06 in decimal form)
- **Years**: 15 years

Now, we multiply Rahul's current monthly expenses by (1 + inflation rate) raised to the power of the number of years:

- **Future Expenses** = ₹70,000 × (1 + 0.06) ^ 15
- **Future Expenses** ≈ ₹70,000 × 2.396
- **Future Expenses** ≈ ₹1,68,000 per month

So, Rahul's estimated monthly expenses in 15 years, adjusted for inflation, will be approximately ₹1,68,000.

Step 2: Calculate Annual Future Expenses

To estimate the total amount Rahul will need to cover his expenses annually, we multiply his future monthly expenses by 12 (since there are 12 months in a year):

- **Annual Expenses** = ₹1,68,000 × 12
- **Annual Expenses** = ₹20,16,000

Rahul will need ₹20.16 lakh annually to cover his living expenses in 15 years.

Step 3: Calculate Required Retirement Corpus Using the 4% Rule

Now, to determine how much total savings Rahul needs by the time he retires, we use the **4% rule**, which suggests that you can safely withdraw 4% of your retirement corpus every year without depleting it. To calculate the required retirement corpus, we multiply the annual expenses by 25 (since 1 divided by 0.04 equals 25):

- **Required Corpus** = Annual Expenses × 25
- **Required Corpus** = ₹20,16,000 × 25
- **Required Corpus** = ₹5.04 crore

Therefore, Rahul needs to accumulate a retirement corpus of **₹5.04 crore** to retire in 15 years and cover his future living expenses.

Rahul's Investment Strategy

To achieve his goal of ₹5.04 crore in 15 years, Rahul decides to follow an investment plan:

1. **Invest ₹50,000 per month in equity mutual funds**, targeting an annual **12% compounded annual growth rate (CAGR)**. This means Rahul expects his investments to grow at 12% each year, on average.
2. **Maintain a diversified portfolio**:
   - 70% in **equity (stocks or equity mutual funds)** for higher growth potential.
   - 20% in **fixed-income instruments (bonds or debt mutual funds)** for stability and lower risk.
   - 10% in **gold** for diversification and to hedge against inflation.
3. **Build an emergency fund** of ₹20 lakh to cover unexpected expenses and provide financial security in case of emergencies.

Summary of Rahul's Plan:

- **Current monthly expenses**: ₹70,000
- **Future monthly expenses in 15 years**: ₹1,68,000
- **Annual future expenses**: ₹20,16,000
- **Required retirement corpus**: ₹5.04 crore

- **Investment Strategy**:
  - ₹50,000/month in equity mutual funds
  - Diversified portfolio: 70% equity, 20% fixed income, 10% gold
  - ₹20 lakh emergency fund

By following this plan and staying disciplined with his savings and investments, Rahul can achieve his goal of retiring early and becoming financially independent by the age of 4

By following this disciplined approach, Rahul is on track to achieve financial independence and retire early.

Income Streams for Financial Independence

Achieving financial independence (FI) involves creating a sustainable flow of income streams that can support your lifestyle, either through passive or active income. These streams ensure you can cover your expenses while building wealth for the future.

1. **Passive Income: The Key to Financial Independence**

   Passive income refers to earnings that require minimal ongoing effort. These streams can provide steady cash flow, reducing reliance on active work. Below are some common passive income sources:

   a. Dividends from Investments

   Dividends are regular payments from stocks, mutual funds, or REITs. Companies distribute a portion of their profits to shareholders as dividends.

Example:

- Investment: ₹10 lakh in high-dividend-yielding stocks with an annual yield of 4%.
- Annual Dividend Income = ₹10,00,000 × 0.04 = ₹40,000.
- With a diversified portfolio, this amount can grow as companies increase dividend payouts over time.

How to Start:

1. Research dividend-paying companies or mutual funds.
2. Invest in consistent performers like HDFC Bank, Infosys, or dividend-focused mutual funds.

b. Rental Income

Real estate is a popular choice for generating passive income. Renting out property can provide consistent cash flow while your property value appreciates over time.

Example:

- Property Value: ₹50 lakh apartment.
- Monthly Rent: ₹15,000 (₹1,80,000 annually).
- Expenses: ₹20,000/year for maintenance and property tax.
- Net Annual Income = ₹1,80,000 - ₹20,000 = ₹1,60,000.

Benefits:

1. Dual income: Rent and capital appreciation.
2. Hedge against inflation.

Tip: Use REITs (Real Estate Investment Trusts) if you cannot afford to buy property outright. They provide exposure to real estate with smaller investments.

c. Business Ventures and Royalties

Starting a business or licensing intellectual property can generate passive income.

Example:

- A software engineer writes an app and licenses it to a company.
- Revenue: ₹5,00,000 upfront and ₹50,000/year in royalties for 10 years.

Small-Scale Business Idea:

- Opening a local tiffin service with ₹50,000 initial investment.
- Monthly profit = ₹10,000.

How to Start: Identify niches like e-commerce, digital courses, or small manufacturing ventures.

2. **Active Income: Balancing Work and FI**

Active income requires direct involvement, typically through a job, freelancing, or consulting. The key to leveraging active income for FI is efficient management and maximizing savings.

a. Working for a Living While Saving Aggressively

Active income provides the seed capital to create passive income streams.

b. Freelancing and Consulting for Supplemental Income

Freelancing in your field of expertise can provide additional income.

By saving her freelance income, she builds a ₹10 lakh emergency fund in just 4 years.

Popular Freelance Fields:

1. Content writing
2. Web development
3. Graphic design
4. Financial consulting

c. Transitioning from Active to Passive Income

As your passive income grows, you can reduce reliance on active work.

Blending Active and Passive Income for FI

1. **Dual-Income Approach:**
   - Continue active work while investing aggressively in passive streams.

     Example: Save bonuses or increments directly into SIPs or real estate.
2. **Reinvest Passive Income:**
   - Use dividends or rental income to buy more assets.

     Example: ₹50,000 annual dividends reinvested in mutual funds grow to ₹5 lakh in 10 years at 12% CAGR.
3. **Automate Finances:**
   - Automate SIPs and investments to avoid lifestyle inflation.

Example: Set up automatic deductions for SIPs on your salary date.

Indian Case Study: Building Dual Income Streams

Profile:

- *Neha Verma,* 35, HR professional, New Delhi.

Active Income:

- ₹1,00,000/month from her job.

Passive Income Plan:

1. Invest ₹25,000/month in SIPs for 15 years at 12% CAGR.
    - Corpus after 15 years: ₹1 crore.
    - Generates ₹8,000/month via SWP (Systematic Withdrawal Plan).
2. Buy a ₹60 lakh property using home loan EMIs of ₹30,000/- month.
    - Rent after 20 years: ₹25,000/- month.

Result:

- By 50, her passive income (₹33,000/- month) replaces a significant portion of her active income.

Cutting Down Expenses for Accelerated Wealth-Building

Reducing expenses is one of the most effective ways to accelerate wealth-building and achieve financial independence. By practicing frugality and avoiding lifestyle inflation, you can save and invest a significant portion of your income, compounding wealth faster over time.

1. **How Frugality and Saving a Large Percentage of Income Accelerates Wealth-Building**

   Frugality doesn't mean deprivation; it means optimizing your spending and focusing on value. The goal is to create a high savings rate, which significantly shortens the time required to achieve financial independence.

   Why Saving More Works

   - Saving a higher percentage of income increases the amount available for investment.
   - Investments generate returns over time, and compounding accelerates the growth.

   Mathematical Example: Savings Rate Impact

   - **Person A** saves 20% of their ₹1,00,000 monthly income, or ₹20,000, and invests it.
   - **Person B** saves 50%, or ₹50,000/month.
   - Assuming a 10% annual return on investments:
   - **Person A:** ₹20,000/month grows to ₹50 lakh in 15 years.
   - **Person B:** ₹50,000/month grows to ₹1.25 crore in the same time.

   By saving a larger percentage, Person B reaches financial independence much faster.

2. **Tips on Reducing Lifestyle Inflation**

   Lifestyle inflation happens when increased income leads to higher spending on luxuries or non-essential items. By keeping lifestyle inflation in check, you can save more and avoid unnecessary financial stress.

a. Recognize Needs vs. Wants

Differentiate between necessities (rent, groceries) and discretionary expenses (dining out, gadgets).

Example: Instead of upgrading to the latest smartphone every year, consider using your current phone for at least three years. Savings = ₹30,000/year.

b. Adopt Budgeting Techniques

Track your income and expenses to identify areas for reduction.

Budgeting Tools:

- Apps like YNAB (You Need A Budget) or Mint.
- The 50/30/20 rule:
  - 50% on needs, 30% on wants, 20% on savings/ investments.
  - Adjust to prioritize savings (e.g., 30/10/60).

Example: If your income is ₹1,00,000/month:

- Needs: ₹30,000
- Wants: ₹10,000
- Savings: ₹60,000

c. Embrace Minimalism

Minimalism focuses on owning fewer, high-value items rather than cluttering your life with unnecessary things.

Example: Instead of buying 10 pairs of shoes, invest in 2-3 versatile, durable pairs. This approach saves money and space.

d. Reduce Housing Costs

Housing often takes up a significant portion of income.

Ways to Save:

- Live in a less expensive locality.
- Share rent with roommates or family.
- Negotiate rent with landlords for long-term leases.

Example:

- Monthly rent = ₹20,000.
- Sharing with a roommate = ₹10,000.
- Annual savings = ₹1,20,000.

e. Control Food and Dining Expenses

Eating out frequently can add up quickly.

Alternatives:

- Cook at home. A meal at home costs ₹50-₹100 compared to ₹300-₹500 at a restaurant.
- Use meal planning to reduce food waste.

Example:

- Dining out thrice a week = ₹6,000/month.
- Cooking at home = ₹2,000/month.
- Monthly savings = ₹4,000.

f. Limit Transportation Costs

Optimize travel to save on fuel and maintenance costs.

Tips:

- Use public transport or carpool.
- Switch to a fuel-efficient or electric vehicle.
- Walk or cycle for short distances.

Example:

- Monthly car fuel cost = ₹8,000.
- Using metro/bus = ₹2,500.
- Monthly savings = ₹5,500.

g. Avoid Subscription Overload

Cancel subscriptions you don't use regularly, like streaming services, gym memberships, or magazine subscriptions.

Example:

- Streaming platforms (Netflix, Amazon Prime, Disney+): ₹1,500/month.
- Retain one platform = ₹500/month.
- Savings = ₹1,000/month or ₹12,000/year.

h. DIY Whenever Possible

Learn to do simple tasks yourself instead of outsourcing.

Example:

- Home cleaning service = ₹3,000/month.
- DIY cleaning = ₹0.
- Annual savings = ₹36,000.

i. Use Cashback and Discounts

Leverage credit card rewards, cashback apps, and discounts for essential purchases.

Example:

- Monthly grocery bill = ₹5,000.
- Cashback offers (5%) = ₹250/month.
- Annual savings = ₹3,000.

Key Takeaways for Expense Cutting:

1. Practice mindful spending by prioritizing needs over wants.
2. Use tools like budgets and apps to track and reduce unnecessary expenses.

3. Embrace frugal habits that align with your financial goals.

   By cutting down expenses and avoiding lifestyle inflation, you can significantly accelerate your journey to financial independence.

Tax Optimization Strategies

Tax optimization is a critical component of wealth-building, as minimizing taxes means more of your income and returns stay with you, allowing them to grow. In the journey toward financial independence (FI), reducing your tax liability becomes essential, especially as your wealth grows. By utilizing tax-saving instruments, you can boost your savings, reduce taxable income, and ultimately accelerate your wealth accumulation.

1. **How Tax-Saving Instruments like NPS, EPF, and PPF Can Boost Savings**

   Various tax-saving instruments provide a great opportunity to save on taxes while simultaneously building your wealth. Here's how three of the most popular instruments—**NPS (National Pension Scheme)**, **EPF (Employees' Provident Fund)**, and **PPF (Public Provident Fund)**—can help:

   A. National Pension Scheme (NPS)

   The **NPS** is a government-backed pension scheme designed to provide income after retirement. Apart from being an excellent retirement tool, NPS also offers attractive tax benefits.

B. Employees' Provident Fund (EPF)

The **EPF** is a mandatory retirement savings plan for salaried employees, where both the employee and employer contribute a certain percentage of the employee's salary each month.

C. Public Provident Fund (PPF)

The **PPF** is one of the safest long-term investment options, backed by the government. It offers tax-free returns, making it a favored choice for conservative investors.

2. **The Importance of Minimizing Tax Liability in the Journey to Financial Independence (FI)**

Minimizing tax liability is essential in the journey to financial independence (FI), as taxes can significantly erode your wealth over time. The more you save on taxes, the more you can reinvest into your portfolio, accelerating your path to FI.

Here's why tax optimization is crucial:

- **Higher Investment Potential**: By reducing your taxable income, you can increase the amount you have to invest. The more you invest, the more your wealth can grow, thanks to the power of compounding.
- **Maximized Returns**: Tax-efficient investments ensure that you retain a larger portion of your returns, instead of paying them out as taxes. For example, by investing in tax-free options like PPF or NPS, the entire return (or a significant portion) remains with you.

- **Long-Term Wealth Building**: The cumulative benefit of tax optimization is especially significant in long-term investments. Reducing taxes at the start gives your investments a greater opportunity to grow without tax erosion, ultimately leading to a larger retirement corpus or early FI.
- **Tax on Capital Gains**: When you invest in equity or mutual funds, taxes on long-term capital gains (LTCG) and short-term capital gains (STCG) may apply. Minimizing taxes in these areas through tax-saving instruments or tax-efficient investment strategies (like holding for the long term to avail of LTCG benefits) is crucial in boosting your savings.

Maintaining Financial Discipline

Financial discipline is a cornerstone of successful wealth-building. It's the ability to manage money wisely, consistently save and invest, and avoid the temptations of unnecessary spending. In your journey to financial independence (FI), maintaining financial discipline is crucial because it ensures that you're always working toward your long-term goals, even in the face of short-term distractions.

1. **Building Habits That Ensure Continuous Wealth-Building**

   Creating and maintaining the right financial habits is essential for consistent wealth-building. Here's how you can build those habits:

A. Pay Yourself First

One of the best habits for wealth-building is to pay yourself first, which means prioritizing savings and investments before spending on anything else. This ensures that you are always saving for the future, regardless of how much you spend in the present.

How to Implement It:

- Set up automated transfers to savings or investment accounts as soon as you receive your income.
- Treat savings and investments as fixed expenses, just like paying bills. By making saving a non-negotiable priority, you ensure that you're consistently putting money aside for your future.

B. Budgeting and Tracking Expenses

A well-structured budget is a powerful tool in maintaining financial discipline. By tracking where your money goes, you can identify areas where you might be overspending and reallocate those funds toward your wealth-building goals.

How to Implement It:

- Create a monthly budget that divides your income into categories like savings, living expenses, and discretionary spending.
- Track all your expenses and analyze them regularly to find areas where you can cut back and save more.
- Use budgeting apps or tools to automate the process and stay on top of your spending.

C. Regularly Review and Adjust Your Investment Plan

As your financial situation evolves, so should your investment plan. Regularly reviewing your investments helps ensure that you are staying on track with your goals and making necessary adjustments based on market conditions or life changes.

How to Implement It:

- Set aside time to review your investment portfolio quarterly or annually.
- If your goals change, or if you experience a significant life event (such as a promotion, marriage, or the birth of a child), adjust your savings or investment contributions accordingly.
- Stay informed about market trends, but don't panic in the face of short-term market fluctuations.

D. Emergency Fund

An emergency fund is essential for avoiding unnecessary debt and financial stress during unexpected circumstances (such as medical emergencies or job loss). Having a well-established emergency fund allows you to focus on long-term wealth-building without being derailed by short-term financial setbacks.

How to Implement It:

- Aim to build an emergency fund equivalent to 3-6 months of living expenses.
- Keep this fund in a liquid, low-risk account, such as a savings account or a short-term debt fund.

E. Consistent Contributions to Retirement Accounts

One of the most powerful wealth-building habits is to contribute regularly to retirement accounts (like NPS, EPF, or PPF). These accounts offer tax advantages and can grow over time, securing your financial future.

How to Implement It:

- Set up automatic contributions to retirement accounts each month.
- Treat retirement savings as a long-term goal that takes precedence over short-term spending.

2. **How to Stay on Track with Long-Term Goals Amidst Short-Term Distractions**

In today's world, distractions are everywhere, and it's easy to get caught up in short-term pleasures or external pressures. Staying focused on long-term goals requires mental discipline and strategies to avoid being swayed by immediate gratification.

A. Visualize Your Financial Independence Goal

Visualization is a powerful tool to help you stay focused on long-term goals. When you can clearly picture what financial independence looks like—whether it's early retirement, starting your own business, or simply having the financial freedom to live life on your terms—it becomes easier to ignore distractions that don't align with that vision.

How to Implement It:

- Create a vision board or write down your financial goals.

- Break down your long-term goals into smaller, achievable milestones and celebrate when you hit those milestones.

B. Stay Focused on the Big Picture

It's easy to get distracted by temporary opportunities or short-term rewards, but these can often derail long-term wealth-building efforts. For example, buying a new car on credit or taking a lavish vacation on a loan might feel good in the short run, but they can create financial strain and take away from future savings.

How to Implement It:

- Remind yourself regularly of the importance of long-term goals.
- Use budgeting apps to set and track financial goals, ensuring that every spending decision aligns with your long-term plans.

C. Set Clear, Specific Financial Goals

Having specific, measurable goals is a great way to maintain focus. Vague goals like "I want to save more money" are difficult to achieve, but specific goals like "I want to save ₹5 lakh for a down payment in 3 years" provide a clear target and roadmap.

How to Implement It:

- Break down larger goals (like achieving FI) into smaller, actionable steps.
- Set deadlines for each goal to keep yourself accountable.

D. Avoid Lifestyle Inflation

As your income increases, there's often a temptation to spend more—this is known as lifestyle inflation. It's important to resist this urge, especially if your goal is to build wealth. Instead, continue living within your means and direct any extra income toward your savings or investments.

How to Implement It:

- When you receive a raise or a bonus, consider allocating a significant portion of it toward savings or investments rather than upgrading your lifestyle.

E. Keep Track of Progress and Celebrate Milestones

Tracking your progress is motivating and can help you stay on track. By regularly assessing how far you've come, you can remind yourself of the benefits of financial discipline.

How to Implement It:

- Use apps to track your savings, investments, and net worth.
- Celebrate small victories, like reaching a savings milestone or successfully sticking to your budget for a month.

4

Understanding Mutual Funds: A Practical Guide for Investors

Mutual funds are a popular and effective investment vehicle for both new and experienced investors. They allow you to pool your money with other investors to gain exposure to a diversified portfolio of assets, including stocks, bonds, and other financial instruments. Understanding the basics and selecting the right mutual fund can significantly boost your investment journey.

1. What Are Mutual Funds?

Mutual funds are collective investment vehicles that pool money from multiple investors and invest it in a variety of securities such as stocks, bonds, money market instruments, or other assets. By pooling money together, these funds allow individuals to access a diversified portfolio, which would be hard to achieve on their own with smaller amounts of capital.

A. How Mutual Funds Pool Money from Many Investors to Invest in Stocks, Bonds, and Other Assets

A mutual fund collects money from numerous investors who share a common investment goal. The fund manager uses this pooled capital to buy securities based on the fund's investment objective, which could be growth, income, or a combination of both.

- **Example**: Let's say 100 investors decide to invest in a mutual fund, and each investor contributes ₹1 lakh. This means the total corpus of the mutual fund is ₹1 crore. The professional fund manager will then allocate this ₹1 crore into a diversified mix of assets based on the type of fund. For example:
  - The manager might invest ₹40 lakhs in stocks of different companies, ₹30 lakhs in bonds, and ₹30 lakhs in government securities. This diversification helps reduce risk while targeting both growth (through equities) and stability (through bonds).
- Once the investments are made, each investor in the mutual fund receives units in the fund, proportional to their contribution. So, if you invested ₹1 lakh in a ₹1 crore fund, you would own 1% of the total units of the fund. The value of these units fluctuates with the performance of the underlying assets. If the value of the fund goes up, the value of your units increases as well.

B. Advantages: Diversification, Professional Management, and Lower Costs

1. **Diversification**: Mutual funds provide diversification by investing in multiple asset classes—stocks, bonds, and others—across various industries and sectors. Diversification helps to spread risk. For example, if a

particular stock in the fund performs poorly, the negative impact on the overall portfolio is reduced because the fund is also invested in other stocks and bonds.

- **Example**: Consider a diversified equity mutual fund that holds stocks in various sectors like technology, pharmaceuticals, and automobiles. If the pharmaceutical sector faces a downturn due to regulatory changes, the loss may be offset by gains in the technology sector or automotive sector, preventing large losses for the investors.

2. **Professional Management**: Mutual funds are managed by experienced fund managers who have the expertise and knowledge to make informed investment decisions. These managers analyze the market, conduct research, and choose the right assets for the fund based on its objectives and prevailing market conditions.
   - **Example**: Suppose there's an economic downturn, and the stock market is underperforming. A professional fund manager may reduce the fund's exposure to high-risk stocks and increase its allocation to bonds or other safer assets, protecting the investor's capital from further decline. This kind of expertise may not be available to an individual investor who is not familiar with the nuances of the market.
3. **Lower Costs**: Mutual funds have the advantage of scale, meaning they can purchase securities in larger quantities at lower transaction costs. If an individual investor were to make the same investments on their own, they would

incur higher costs in terms of brokerage fees, research, and management.

- **Example**: If you were to buy shares of 50 different companies on your own, you would have to pay a separate transaction fee for each trade. However, a mutual fund can buy these stocks at a bulk rate, which lowers the overall transaction cost for investors. Additionally, fund managers handle all the administrative tasks, saving you time and effort.

> *"The investor's chief problem—and even his worst enemy—is likely to be himself."*
> —Benjamin Graham, *The Intelligent Investor*

2. Types of Mutual Funds

Mutual funds come in various types, catering to different risk profiles and investment objectives. The primary types are equity funds, debt funds, and hybrid funds. Each type has its characteristics in terms of risk, return, and suitability for different investors.

A. Equity Mutual Funds: High-Risk, High-Return Funds That Invest in Stocks

Equity mutual funds are one of the most popular investment vehicles for individuals looking to invest in the stock market without directly picking individual stocks. These funds primarily invest in equities or stocks, making them suitable for investors with a high risk tolerance and a long-term investment horizon. Below is a detailed explanation of equity mutual funds, along with examples, risk-return dynamics, and suitability for different types of investors.

What Are Equity Mutual Funds?

Equity mutual funds pool money from multiple investors and invest primarily in the stock market (equities). The main goal of equity funds is **capital appreciation**—to grow the value of the investment by buying stocks of companies that are expected to increase in value over time. These funds are managed by professional fund managers who actively select the stocks based on the fund's investment strategy.

- **Example**: A fund like **SBI Bluechip Fund** primarily invests in large-cap stocks, which are the top 100 companies by market capitalization. These are well-established companies, often leaders in their sectors, such as **Reliance Industries**, **HDFC Bank**, or **Tata Consultancy Services** (TCS).

Risk Profile of Equity Mutual Funds

Equity funds are considered **high-risk investments** because stock prices can be volatile and fluctuate significantly. Here's how:

- **Volatility**: The value of stocks can change rapidly due to several factors such as market conditions, company performance, economic news, political events, and global factors. This can lead to significant fluctuations in the value of an equity mutual fund in the short term.

- **Market Corrections and Recessions**: During market corrections or economic downturns, even well-established companies can see their stock prices drop. The overall market trend can impact individual stocks, even if the underlying company is fundamentally strong.

Risk Example: If you invest in an equity mutual fund like SBI Bluechip Fund, the stock prices of companies like **Reliance Industries** or **HDFC Bank** can fluctuate heavily based on market sentiment, even though these are stable, large-cap companies. For instance:

- During a market boom, the prices of these stocks could rise sharply (e.g., 20% in a year).
- During a market correction, the prices could drop (e.g., by 10-15% in a short period).

This high risk is typically the trade-off for the potential of high returns.

Return Potential of Equity Mutual Funds

Equity funds offer **high return potential**, but this comes with the risk of volatility. Historically, equity funds have provided higher returns over the long term compared to other types of mutual funds, such as debt or hybrid funds.

- **Long-Term Growth**: Over the long term (5 to 10 years or more), stock markets tend to show a general upward trend, and equity mutual funds can generate attractive returns.
- **Higher Potential Returns**: Equity funds invest in growth-oriented stocks, which have the potential to

provide higher returns, especially in a bull market (when stock prices are rising).

Return Example: Let's take the **SBI Bluechip Fund** as an example:

- **In a Bull Market**: If the market is experiencing a strong upward trend, the value of stocks like **Reliance Industries** or **HDFC Bank** might rise significantly. For example, if the market rises by 15-20% in a year, the equity fund could see returns of 18-22% (because the fund's large-cap stocks are likely to follow the market trend).
- **In a Market Correction**: If there's a market correction or economic downturn, the same stocks could lose 10-15% of their value. For example, during a recession, **Reliance Industries** could see a 12% drop, and the equity fund could mirror this decline.

Suitability of Equity Mutual Funds

Equity mutual funds are suitable for investors who meet the following criteria:

- **High-Risk Tolerance**: Since the value of equity mutual funds can fluctuate significantly, these funds are best suited for investors who are comfortable with high levels of risk.
- **Long-Term Investment Horizon (5-10 years or more)**: Equity funds are better suited for long-term investors because they provide the potential for high returns over time. The longer your investment

horizon, the more time you have to ride out market volatility and take advantage of compound growth.

- **Growth-Oriented Financial Goals**: Investors who are looking for higher growth potential and are focused on building wealth over the long term (e.g., retirement, child's education) would benefit from investing in equity mutual funds.

Example: Let's say you have a 10-year investment horizon and are saving for retirement. You are willing to accept the possibility of short-term volatility in exchange for higher long-term returns. In this case, investing in an equity mutual fund like **SBI Bluechip Fund** makes sense. Over 10 years, the growth potential of this fund could significantly outpace inflation and provide a larger corpus for your retirement.

Key Features of Equity Mutual Funds

- **High Risk, High Return**: The primary feature of equity funds is their potential for high returns, but they come with significant volatility. Equity funds can offer returns of 12-18% per annum over the long term, depending on market conditions and the fund's portfolio.
- **Capital Appreciation**: Equity funds focus on increasing the value of your investment by selecting stocks with strong growth potential. Unlike debt funds that provide interest income, equity funds aim to appreciate the capital invested.

- **Active Fund Management**: In actively managed equity funds, a fund manager selects the stocks based on research, market trends, and economic conditions. In contrast, passive funds (like index funds) track a market index, such as the Nifty 50 or Sensex, and invest in the stocks in that index.

Example of Equity Mutual Fund Investment: SBI Bluechip Fund

Let's break down an example to illustrate how equity mutual funds work:

Scenario 1: Bull Market (Market Growth)

- You invest ₹1 lakh in **SBI Bluechip Fund**.
- The fund has a portfolio mainly consisting of large-cap stocks like **Reliance Industries**, **HDFC Bank**, and **Tata Consultancy Services** (TCS).
- Over the course of the year, due to strong market conditions and a boom in sectors such as technology and energy, these stocks rise significantly.
- **Fund Performance**: The fund's overall return is 20%, meaning your ₹1 lakh investment grows to ₹1.20 lakh.

Scenario 2: Market Correction (Market Decline)

- The same ₹1 lakh investment in **SBI Bluechip Fund** is made, but now there is a market correction, and the stock prices of **Reliance Industries**, **HDFC Bank**, and **TCS** fall.
- The fund's value declines by 12%, and the value of your ₹1 lakh investment drops to ₹88,000.

B. Debt Funds: Lower-Risk Funds Investing in Government and Corporate Bonds

Debt mutual funds are designed for conservative investors seeking stability and relatively lower levels of risk. Unlike equity funds, which invest primarily in stocks, debt funds focus on fixed-income securities such as **government bonds**, **corporate bonds**, and other debt instruments. These funds aim to provide regular income with relatively lower volatility compared to equities, making them suitable for individuals with a lower risk tolerance.

Let's explore the key features of **debt mutual funds**, including their risk profile, return potential, and suitability for various types of investors.

What Are Debt Mutual Funds?

Debt mutual funds pool money from multiple investors and invest primarily in debt instruments. The main goal of debt funds is to generate **fixed income** for investors, typically through interest payments on the bonds they hold. These funds invest in a variety of debt securities, including:

- **Government Bonds**: Debt securities issued by the government, considered very low-risk because they are backed by the government's credit.
- **Corporate Bonds**: Debt securities issued by companies. These carry a higher risk than government bonds but offer higher interest rates.
- **Money Market Instruments**: Short-term debt securities such as treasury bills or commercial papers, often used for liquidity management in debt funds.

Risk Profile of Debt Mutual Funds

Debt mutual funds are generally **low to moderate risk investments** compared to equity funds, depending on the types of debt instruments they hold. Here's a breakdown of the risk involved:

- **Government Bonds**: These are considered **low-risk** because they are issued by the government, which is unlikely to default. Bonds from stable governments (such as the Indian government) are the safest in terms of principal repayment and interest payments.
- **Corporate Bonds**: These carry **moderate risk** compared to government bonds. The level of risk depends on the **credit rating** of the issuing company. For example, bonds issued by large, stable companies like **Tata** or **Reliance** are considered less risky than those issued by smaller, lower-rated companies. The risk is higher because these companies might default on interest payments or the bond's principal amount, especially during difficult economic conditions.
- **Interest Rate Risk**: One of the key risks for debt funds is **interest rate risk**. When interest rates rise, the value of existing bonds falls, which could affect the price of a debt mutual fund's holdings. However, this risk can be minimized by holding bonds until maturity.
- **Credit Risk**: This is the risk that the issuer of a bond will not be able to meet its financial obligations (i.e.,

pay the interest or repay the principal). Debt funds that invest in high-rated bonds are less prone to credit risk.

Return Potential of Debt Mutual Funds

Debt mutual funds typically offer **lower returns** compared to equity funds, but their returns are more stable and predictable. Returns come from **interest income** generated by the bonds in the portfolio. These returns are often higher than those of savings accounts or fixed deposits, but lower than equity funds.

- **Interest Income**: The primary source of return from debt funds is the **interest paid by the bonds** held in the portfolio. For example, a bond with an interest rate of 7% will provide the fund with 7% annual income, which is passed on to the investors.
- **Capital Appreciation**: In addition to interest income, debt funds can experience capital appreciation (increase in the value of bonds) if interest rates fall or if the bonds' credit ratings improve. However, this is not the primary source of returns in debt funds, as the focus is more on stability and income.

Return Example:

- **ICICI Prudential Corporate Bond Fund**, which invests in high-rated corporate bonds and government securities, might offer **returns of around 6-7% per year**. This return is better than what you would get from a traditional savings account or a fixed deposit, but significantly lower than the potential returns from equity funds.

Suitability of Debt Mutual Funds

Debt mutual funds are ideal for investors who are looking for stability, regular income, and lower risk. They are particularly suitable for individuals in the following situations:

- **Conservative Investors**: Investors who are risk-averse and prefer stable, predictable returns with minimal fluctuations would benefit from debt funds.
- **Capital Preservation**: For investors who prioritize the safety of their principal (the original investment amount) over high returns, debt funds are a good choice. Government bonds, in particular, provide a high level of security for the invested amount.
- **Shorter Investment Horizon**: Investors with a short-term investment horizon (1-3 years) who don't want to expose themselves to the volatility of equities would find debt funds attractive. These funds are generally less sensitive to market downturns than equity funds.
- **Investors Nearing Retirement**: Debt funds are ideal for individuals who are nearing retirement and need a stable income source without taking on too much risk. The regular interest payments from bonds can act as a steady income stream.

Example: ICICI Prudential Corporate Bond Fund

To illustrate how a debt mutual fund works, let's take the example of the **ICICI Prudential Corporate Bond**

Fund. This fund primarily invests in high-rated corporate bonds (issued by companies like **Reliance** or **Tata**), along with government securities.

Scenario:

- You invest ₹1 lakh in the **ICICI Prudential Corporate Bond Fund**.
- The fund focuses on bonds offering an annual interest rate of around **7%**.
- Over the course of the year, the fund generates interest income from these bonds, which is distributed to the investors.
- **Return Example**: After one year, the fund might offer a return of **6-7%** on your investment, which means your ₹1 lakh could grow to ₹1.06 lakh or ₹1.07 lakh.

In comparison to **savings accounts** (which may offer 3-4% returns) or **fixed deposits** (typically offering 5-6% returns), debt mutual funds can provide better returns with relatively lower risk.

Advantages of Debt Mutual Funds

1. **Stable Income**: The primary advantage of debt funds is the predictable and steady income generated from bond interest payments.
2. **Lower Risk**: Debt funds are generally less volatile than equity funds and are suitable for conservative investors.
3. **Liquidity**: Unlike traditional fixed deposits, debt mutual funds can be easily redeemed, providing higher liquidity to investors.

4. **Tax Benefits**: Debt funds offer certain tax advantages, especially for long-term investors who hold the fund for over 3 years, as long-term capital gains (LTCG) are taxed at a lower rate (20% with indexation).

Disadvantages of Debt Mutual Funds

1. **Lower Returns**: While debt funds offer lower returns than equity funds, they also carry lower risk. However, they may not provide the growth potential needed for long-term financial goals like retirement.
2. **Interest Rate Risk**: Debt funds can still be affected by changes in interest rates, which can cause the price of the bonds in the portfolio to fluctuate.
3. **Credit Risk**: Investing in corporate bonds can carry some level of risk depending on the issuing company's financial health. If the issuer defaults, the returns from the debt fund could be affected.

C. Hybrid Funds: A Mix of Equity and Debt to Balance Risk and Return

Hybrid funds combine both **equity** (stocks) and **debt** (bonds) instruments in a single portfolio, making them a suitable investment choice for those who seek a balance between growth potential and stability. These funds aim to provide the benefits of both asset classes, with the **growth** potential of equities and the **stability** of debt. By investing in both equities and bonds, hybrid funds help investors balance the risks and rewards associated with each type of asset.

What Are Hybrid Funds?

Hybrid funds typically invest in two types of assets:

1. **Equity (Stocks)**: This portion of the fund provides growth potential. The equity investment is aimed at capital appreciation, which means that the value of the stocks can increase over time. Equities have the potential to offer higher returns, but they are also more volatile, meaning their prices can fluctuate widely based on market conditions.
2. **Debt (Bonds)**: The debt portion of the fund provides stability and regular income through interest payments. Bonds are generally considered safer investments compared to stocks because their prices fluctuate less and provide a predictable return. Bonds in a hybrid fund can include government securities, corporate bonds, and other fixed-income instruments.

The allocation between equity and debt can vary based on the fund's strategy, and different hybrid funds have different risk profiles depending on this allocation.

Risk Profile of Hybrid Funds

Risk Level: Hybrid funds typically have a **moderate risk** level. These funds are less volatile than pure equity funds because they have exposure to bonds, which are less sensitive to market movements. However, the equity portion still exposes the fund to market volatility, meaning the returns can still fluctuate significantly, especially in the short term.

- **Equity Portion**: The equity portion of the fund provides growth opportunities, but it is subject to market fluctuations. If the market is performing well, the value of the equity holdings can increase significantly, but if the market declines, the equity holdings can also lose value.

- **Debt Portion**: The debt portion offers more stability since bonds typically have lower volatility compared to stocks. The value of bonds may fluctuate based on interest rates, inflation, and credit risk, but generally, they offer more predictable returns.

By combining both asset classes, hybrid funds aim to balance the higher volatility of stocks with the more stable, fixed income of bonds, reducing overall risk compared to an equity-only fund.

Return Potential of Hybrid Funds

Return Level: The return on a hybrid fund depends on the performance of both the equity and debt portions. Hybrid funds offer **higher returns** than pure debt funds because of their equity exposure, but they generally offer lower returns than equity funds, as the debt portion limits the growth potential.

- **Equity Returns**: The equity portion of a hybrid fund is designed for capital growth. In a strong or bullish market, the equity portion can generate substantial returns, leading to a higher overall return for the fund.
- **Debt Returns**: The debt portion of the fund provides more stable returns through regular interest payments. These returns are usually more predictable and less

volatile than equities, making them a stabilizing factor in the fund's overall performance.

In general, hybrid funds offer a **balanced return**, which means they are likely to provide a return that is **higher** than that of pure debt funds but **lower** than that of pure equity funds. Historically, hybrid funds have delivered annual returns in the range of **8-12%**, although this can vary based on market conditions and the fund's asset allocation.

> "Do not save what is left after spending, but spend what is left after saving."
>
> **—Warren Buffett**

Suitability of Hybrid Funds

Hybrid funds are ideal for investors who seek a balance between risk and return. They are suitable for those who want to invest in equities but are also concerned about the risks associated with market volatility. Hybrid funds provide the **growth potential** of equities while offering the **stability** of debt, making them suitable for investors with a **medium-term investment horizon** (typically **3-5 years**).

They are also appropriate for investors who have a **moderate risk tolerance**. If you are not willing to take on the full volatility of the stock market but still want to achieve higher returns than what debt funds offer, hybrid funds may be a good choice.

Furthermore, hybrid funds are suitable for investors looking for **diversification**. They provide built-in diversification by investing in both stocks and bonds, helping to spread the risk across different asset classes.

Example: HDFC Hybrid Equity Fund

Consider the **HDFC Hybrid Equity Fund**, which is an example of an aggressive hybrid fund. This fund typically invests about **60-70%** of its portfolio in **equities** and the remaining **30-40%** in **debt instruments** (such as government bonds and high-rated corporate bonds).

Scenario 1: Bullish Market

In a **bullish market**, where the stock market is performing well:

- The equity portion of the fund may appreciate by 15-20% in a year, as the stocks in the portfolio rise in value.
- The debt portion of the fund may generate stable returns of **6-7%** due to interest payments on bonds.
- As a result, the fund's overall return could be around **12-15%**, benefiting from the strong performance of equities, along with steady returns from the debt portion.

Scenario 2: Bearish Market

In a **bearish market**, where the stock market is facing a downturn:

- The equity portion of the fund may decline by **10-15%**, as the stock prices fall.
- The debt portion, however, will continue to provide a **6-7%** return through interest payments on bonds.

- Thanks to the stability provided by the debt portion, the overall fund decline may be more modest, around **3-5%**, compared to a purely equity fund, which could experience much larger losses in a market downturn.

Advantages of Hybrid Funds

1. **Diversification**: Hybrid funds provide automatic diversification by investing in both stocks and bonds, which can reduce the risk associated with being heavily invested in one asset class. This diversification helps balance out the impact of market fluctuations.
2. **Moderate Risk**: These funds offer a more moderate risk profile compared to equity funds. While the equity portion can lead to volatility, the debt portion helps to cushion the effects of market downturns.
3. **Steady Returns**: The debt component provides stable returns through interest payments, while the equity component offers growth potential. This combination allows hybrid funds to provide a balance between capital appreciation and regular income.
4. **Flexibility**: Hybrid funds offer flexibility for investors with a **medium-term investment horizon**. They can provide growth during bullish market periods, while also offering stability during market corrections.

Disadvantages of Hybrid Funds

1. **Limited Upside Potential**: While hybrid funds are balanced, they may not provide the same high returns as equity-only funds during a strong bull market. The debt portion of the fund limits the overall growth potential.

2. **Complex Asset Allocation**: The asset allocation between equity and debt is managed by the fund manager, and it may not always be aligned with the investor's risk preferences or market conditions. This requires monitoring the fund to ensure it continues to match your investment goals.
3. **Exposure to Market Risk**: Although hybrid funds are less volatile than equity funds, they are still exposed to market risk. The equity portion can lead to significant declines during market downturns, and while the debt portion can provide stability, it cannot fully protect against large market corrections.

In investing, what is comfortable is rarely profitable."

— **Robert Arnott**, Investment Manager and Economist

3. **How to Select a Mutual Fund**

Selecting the right mutual fund is crucial to achieving your financial goals. With so many funds available, it's important to consider several key factors to ensure the fund aligns with your investment objectives, risk tolerance, and investment horizon.

A. Key Factors to Consider in Mutual Fund Selection

When choosing a mutual fund, it's important to evaluate various factors that can significantly impact your investment returns. These factors include **fund performance**, **expense ratio**, **fund manager's track**

record, and **risk level**. Understanding each of these elements will help you make informed decisions and align your investments with your financial goals and risk tolerance.

1. **Fund Performance**

   The performance of a mutual fund is perhaps the most critical factor to assess before investing. While past performance does not guarantee future results, reviewing a fund's historical returns helps you understand how it has performed during various market conditions.

   How to Evaluate Fund Performance

   To evaluate a mutual fund's performance, compare it with its **benchmark index** (such as the Nifty 50 for Indian equity funds) and its **peers** in the same category. For example, when looking at an equity fund, you can compare it with other equity funds in the same **large-cap** category. A fund that consistently outperforms its benchmark and peers suggests that the fund manager has been successful in selecting stocks that perform better than the broader market.

   However, it's equally important to assess how the fund performed during **market corrections** or periods of downturn. Some funds may deliver impressive returns in a bull market but underperform or experience steep losses during market corrections. A fund with high volatility and large drawdowns may not suit investors with a lower risk tolerance.

Example: Consider the **SBI Bluechip Fund**, which primarily invests in large-cap stocks. Suppose the fund has consistently outperformed the **Nifty 50 index** by 2-3% over the past 5 years. This indicates that the fund manager has successfully identified stocks that outperformed the overall market. However, it is important to check how the fund performed during periods of market downturns, such as during the COVID-19 market crash. If the fund experienced significant losses during such corrections, it may indicate a higher risk level, which might not be suitable for more conservative investors.

2. **Expense Ratio**

The **expense ratio** is the annual fee that the mutual fund charges to manage its assets. It covers the costs of running the fund, including fund management, administration, and marketing. The expense ratio is expressed as a percentage of the fund's assets and is deducted from the returns generated by the fund.

How to Evaluate Expense Ratio

Generally, a lower expense ratio means that a larger portion of the fund's returns is passed on to the investors. Over the long term, even a small difference in the expense ratio can significantly impact the overall returns. On the other hand, if a fund has an exceptionally high expense ratio, it could erode the returns, especially in low-return market conditions.

Example

Consider two equity funds:

- **Fund A** has an expense ratio of **0.5%**.
- **Fund B** has an expense ratio of **2%**.

Assuming both funds perform similarly, **Fund A** will likely deliver higher **net returns** over the long term due to the lower management fees. Over time, the difference in expenses could add up, making **Fund A** a more cost-efficient choice for investors.

3. **Fund Manager's Track Record**

The expertise and experience of the **fund manager** play a critical role in the performance of a mutual fund. A fund manager's ability to navigate the markets and make sound investment decisions can have a direct impact on the fund's returns.

How to Evaluate Fund Manager's Track Record

When evaluating a mutual fund, research the background of the fund manager, focusing on their experience and track record in managing similar funds. A fund manager who has demonstrated skill in managing funds through different market conditions (both **bull** and **bear markets**) can offer greater stability and confidence to investors.

Example

Consider the **HDFC Top 200 Fund**, which primarily invests in large-cap stocks. If the fund manager has successfully managed similar funds in the past, such as other **large-cap funds**, their experience can be a good indicator of their ability to manage risk and optimize returns. A fund manager who has managed funds through multiple market cycles and delivered consistent returns will likely be able to navigate future market challenges more effectively.

4. **Risk Level**

   The **risk level** of a mutual fund refers to the amount of volatility or uncertainty associated with the returns generated by the fund. Different funds carry different levels of risk based on their **investment strategy** (equity, debt, hybrid). It's crucial to assess your own **risk tolerance** and investment goals before selecting a fund.

   - **Equity funds** generally carry a **high risk** because the stock market can experience significant fluctuations. However, they also have the potential for **higher returns** over the long term.
   - **Debt funds**, on the other hand, are generally **lower risk** since they invest in bonds and other fixed-income securities. They offer more **stable returns** but typically provide lower returns compared to equity funds.
   - **Hybrid funds** balance risk by investing in both equity and debt, offering a middle ground between the two extremes.

   How to Evaluate Risk Level

   Before investing in any mutual fund, assess your **financial goals** and **risk appetite**. If you're looking for long-term growth and can tolerate fluctuations, equity funds may be suitable. On the other hand, if you are nearing retirement or prefer a more stable income stream, debt funds or hybrid funds may be better options.

Example

- If you are **in your 30s** and looking for **long-term growth**, an **equity fund** like the **SBI Bluechip Fund** may be appropriate because you have the time to ride out market volatility and benefit from potential market growth.
- If you are closer to **retirement** or have a **lower risk tolerance**, a **debt fund** like the **ICICI Prudential Corporate Bond Fund** may be more suitable. Debt funds provide stable, predictable returns with less risk of large losses.

B. Rating Agencies like CRISIL and Morningstar Can Help Investors Make Informed Decisions

Rating agencies like **CRISIL** and **Morningstar** play a crucial role in helping investors evaluate and choose mutual funds. These agencies provide independent ratings and research, which can offer valuable insights into a fund's performance, risk profile, management quality, and other key factors. By using the ratings and analyses provided by these agencies, investors can make more informed decisions about where to allocate their money.

1. CRISIL

CRISIL (formerly known as Credit Rating Information Services of India Limited) is a prominent credit rating agency in India that offers ratings and detailed research on various financial instruments, including mutual funds. CRISIL evaluates mutual funds based on multiple parameters such as **risk-adjusted returns**, **portfolio quality**, **expense ratios**, and the **fund manager's track record**. CRISIL's ratings help investors assess the potential of a fund relative to the risk involved, making it easier to compare funds within the same category.

Example:

Let's say you are considering an **equity fund**, like the **ICICI Prudential Bluechip Fund**. If this fund has been assigned a **"CRISIL Fund Rank 1"**, it suggests that, based on CRISIL's analysis, it has demonstrated strong performance in its category, factoring in both **risk** and **return**. This means that the fund has been successful in delivering good returns relative to the level of risk it has taken on, making it a potentially strong investment choice in the equity fund space.

2. **Morningstar**

Morningstar is a globally recognized investment research firm that provides in-depth analysis and ratings for mutual funds, ETFs, and other investment products. Morningstar is known for its **star rating system**, which evaluates mutual funds based on factors such as performance, risk, management quality, and expenses. The rating is a quick way for investors to gauge a fund's past performance, with **5 stars** being the highest rating.

Morningstar also provides detailed reports that assess **risk**, **management effectiveness**, and **expense**

efficiency, helping investors understand not just the returns of a fund but also the strategies used by the fund manager to achieve those returns.

Example:

If you're considering a **hybrid fund**, such as the **HDFC Hybrid Equity Fund**, Morningstar's **star rating** can help you assess the fund's overall performance. Suppose this fund has a **4-star rating**. This means that it has delivered **above-average returns** in comparison to its peers while maintaining an **acceptable level of risk**. A 4-star rating signals that the fund has a strong track record of performance and is considered a solid choice in the hybrid fund category.

How CRISIL and Morningstar Help Investors

1. **Fund Comparison:** Both CRISIL and Morningstar provide comparative data that helps investors assess how a particular fund stacks up against its peers. This allows investors to select the best-performing funds in a given category, based on specific factors such as risk, return, and management quality.
2. **Risk Assessment:** Rating agencies like CRISIL and Morningstar evaluate funds not just on returns but also on the risks involved. This helps investors understand whether the return generated by a fund justifies the level of risk taken. If you are risk-averse, you might prefer a fund with a lower risk profile, even if it means a slightly lower return.
3. **Informed Decision-Making:** These ratings offer investors an objective and detailed perspective on a

fund's performance, which is especially useful for beginners or those looking to diversify their investments. The independent research conducted by CRISIL and Morningstar helps investors avoid funds with poor management or excessive risk.

4. **Monitoring Funds:** Investors can use CRISIL and Morningstar ratings to track the performance of their investments over time. If a fund's rating drops or if the fund's performance declines, it may be a signal for the investor to reconsider their investment or explore other options.

4. SIP vs Lump-Sum Investment

Both Systematic Investment Plans (SIPs) and lump-sum investments are popular ways to invest in mutual funds. However, the approach you choose largely depends on your financial goals, risk tolerance, and market conditions. Let's break down the key differences, along with their pros and cons, to help you understand which option is best suited for you.

A. Pros and Cons of SIPs vs Lump-Sum Investments

When deciding how to invest in mutual funds, two common approaches are **Systematic Investment Plans (SIPs)** and **Lump-Sum Investments**. Each method has its own set of advantages and disadvantages, and the right choice depends on your financial goals, risk tolerance, and market conditions.

SIPs (Systematic Investment Plan)

SIPs involve investing a fixed amount of money regularly into mutual funds, typically on a monthly or quarterly basis.

Pros of SIPs:

1. **Disciplined Investing:**
    - SIPs promote regular, disciplined investing, helping to create a habit of saving.
    - This approach is particularly helpful for those who find it difficult to make large, one-time investments.
    - By committing to fixed monthly contributions, you ensure consistent investing, even during market fluctuations.
    - **Example:** If you invest ₹5,000 every month in an equity mutual fund, your habit of saving becomes ingrained, and you stay on track with your financial goals, even during volatile market periods.
2. **Rupee Cost Averaging:**
    - SIPs benefit from **rupee cost averaging**. This means that when markets are down, you buy more units, and when markets are up, you buy fewer units. This helps average out the cost of your investment over time and reduces the impact of short-term market volatility.
    - **Example:** If the NAV (Net Asset Value) is ₹100 in the first month, ₹110 in the second, and ₹90 in the third, you'll buy 50, 45.45, and 55.56 units, respectively, averaging the cost and mitigating short-term market swings.

3. **Mitigates Market Timing Risk:**
   - SIPs remove the need to time the market, which is difficult even for seasoned investors. By spreading your investment over time, you reduce the risk of investing at the wrong time (e.g., during a market peak).
   - **Example:** If you invest a large sum during a market peak and the market declines soon after, you might incur losses. With SIPs, you're investing periodically, which reduces the risk of buying at an unfavorable time.

Cons of SIPs:

1. **Returns May Be Lower in a Strong Bull Market:**
   - While SIPs are effective in volatile markets, they may not perform as well during a strong bull market, where a lump-sum investment could capture more gains.
   - **Example:** If the market has been growing steadily for six months and you start an SIP now, you might not benefit as much as someone who made a lump-sum investment six months ago when prices were lower.

Lump-Sum Investment

A lump-sum investment involves investing a large amount of money into a mutual fund at once.

Pros of Lump-Sum Investment:

1. **Beneficial in a Rising Market:**
   - If the market is in an uptrend, lump-sum investments can benefit significantly, as you're investing a larger

amount of money at current prices, potentially leading to higher returns.

- **Example:** If you invest ₹1 lakh in a mutual fund that increases by 15% over the next year, your investment will grow to ₹1.15 lakh. Lump-sum investing allows you to fully capitalize on the market's growth.

2. **Requires Less Ongoing Effort and Decision-Making:**
   - After making a lump-sum investment, you don't need to worry about making regular contributions. This makes it a "set it and forget it" investment strategy.
   - **Example:** If you receive ₹10 lakh as a bonus and invest it all at once, you don't have to track monthly contributions, just monitor the fund's performance periodically.

Cons of Lump-Sum Investment:

1. **Greater Risk If the Market Falls After Investment:**
   - The main drawback of lump-sum investing is the risk of market timing. If the market declines after you make your investment, you could face immediate losses because all your money is exposed to the market at once.
   - **Example:** If you invest ₹1 lakh just before a market downturn of 10%, your investment could lose ₹10,000, whereas SIPs would have spread the risk over time.
2. **Not Ideal for Limited Investment Horizons or Funds:**
   - Lump-sum investments are generally more suited for investors with a significant amount of capital

to invest and a long-term investment horizon. If you have limited funds or a short-term horizon, this approach can be riskier.

- **Example:** If you have ₹10,000 in savings and want to invest, a lump-sum approach might expose you to too much risk in the short term. In this case, SIP would be a safer and more manageable option.

B. When to Choose SIPs for Consistent Growth vs Lump-Sum for Larger Investments

The choice between **SIPs** (Systematic Investment Plans) and **lump-sum investments** depends on various factors, including the amount of money you have to invest, your financial goals, risk tolerance, and the market conditions. Here's when you should consider each option:

1. **Choose SIP:**

   SIPs are a great choice for those looking for consistency, discipline, and lower risk in their investment strategy. Here's when to consider SIPs:

- **When You Want Steady, Long-Term Growth:**
- ➢ SIPs are perfect for long-term wealth accumulation. By investing regularly, you benefit from the power of compounding, and the consistent contributions help you ride out market volatility.
- ➢ **Example:** If you invest ₹5,000 monthly in an equity mutual fund, over time, your contributions grow steadily. Even if markets fluctuate, your long-term returns are generally positive due to rupee cost averaging.

- **For Smaller or Regular Investments:**
  - SIPs work well for individuals with limited capital or those who prefer to make small, regular investments. Even small amounts like ₹1,000 or ₹5,000 per month can compound significantly over time.
  - **Example:** If you invest ₹2,000 each month, you'll accumulate ₹24,000 in a year, plus any potential returns, helping you build wealth gradually without putting a strain on your monthly budget.
- **When You're Risk-Averse or New to Investing:**
  - If you're new to investing or prefer a lower-risk approach, SIPs allow you to invest gradually, reducing the impact of market timing. By spreading your investment across various market conditions, SIPs minimize the risk of entering the market at a peak.
  - **Example:** If you're unsure about the market's direction, SIPs provide the comfort of investing a fixed amount consistently, so you don't have to worry about timing the market. Your purchase price averages out, providing a balanced risk approach.

2. **Choose Lump-Sum:**

   Lump-sum investments are suitable for those who have a larger amount of capital and are confident in the market's growth potential. Here's when lump-sum investing is ideal:

- **If You Have a Large Sum of Money:**
  - If you've received a lump sum through inheritance, a bonus, or other sources, you can take advantage

of lump-sum investments to potentially gain from market growth. This method maximizes the invested amount, especially in favorable market conditions.

- **Example:** If you inherit ₹10 lakh and want to invest it in an equity fund, a lump-sum investment could potentially bring higher returns over time, especially if the market is performing well.

- **When the Market is Poised for Growth:**
  - If the market is in a strong bullish phase, lump-sum investments can yield substantial returns because you're investing a larger sum of money at a time when the market is expected to rise.
  - **Example:** If the market is trending upwards and you invest ₹1 lakh in an equity fund, you can benefit fully from the market's growth without waiting for periodic contributions.

- **When You Have a Long-Term Investment Horizon:**
  - If your financial goal is a long-term one, such as retirement or funding your child's education, lump-sum investments can start benefiting from compounding immediately. The sooner your money is invested, the more time it has to grow.
  - **Example:** If you receive ₹1 lakh as a bonus and the market is in a growth phase, lump-sum investing could help you see quicker growth, as opposed to an SIP, which would spread out the investment over time.

5. **Taxation of Mutual Funds**

Understanding the taxation of mutual funds is essential for maximizing your returns and minimizing your tax liabilities. Taxes on mutual fund investments can be classified into two broad categories: **short-term capital gains (STCG)** and **long-term capital gains (LTCG)**. These taxes vary based on the type of fund (equity or debt), the holding period, and the amount of profit made. Let's deep dive into the details:

A. Taxation of Equity and Debt Funds: Short-Term and Long-Term Capital Gains Tax

1. **Equity Funds: Tax Treatment of Capital Gains**

Equity funds primarily invest in stocks, and the tax treatment of capital gains depends on the holding period of the mutual fund units. Here's how it works:

- **Short-Term Capital Gains (STCG) Tax on Equity Funds:**

- If equity mutual fund units are sold within **1 year** of investment, any profits made are considered **short-term capital gains (STCG)**.
- **Tax Rate:** STCG on equity funds is taxed at **15%**, regardless of your tax bracket.

Example:

- Suppose you invest ₹1 lakh in an equity fund and sell it after **9 months** for ₹1.2 lakh.
- The gain of ₹20,000 is considered short-term capital gain (STCG).
- Tax = 15% of ₹20,000 = ₹3,000.

- Your effective post-tax profit = ₹20,000 - ₹3,000 = **₹17,000**.

- **Long-Term Capital Gains (LTCG) Tax on Equity Funds:**

- If the units of an equity mutual fund are sold after **1 year**, the profits are considered **long-term capital gains (LTCG)**.
- **Tax Rate:** LTCG on equity funds is **10%** for gains above ₹1 lakh in a financial year, with **no indexation benefit**.

Example:

- If you invest ₹1 lakh in an equity mutual fund and sell it after **2 years** for ₹1.5 lakh, your capital gain is ₹50,000.
- Since the gain is **below ₹1 lakh**, there is no LTCG tax.

However, if the gain had been ₹1.2 lakh:

- **Excess gain above ₹1 lakh = ₹20,000**.
- Tax on ₹20,000 = 10% = ₹2,000.
- Your effective post-tax profit = ₹1.2 lakh - ₹2,000 = **₹1.18 lakh**.

Summary:

- **Current STCG Tax** (for holdings less than 1 year) subject to change: **15%** on profits.
- **Current LTCG Tax** (for holdings above 1 year) subject to change: **10%** on profits exceeding ₹1 lakh in a financial year.

Understanding the tax treatment can help you plan your investments more efficiently, especially if you're looking to minimize your tax liabilities while maximizing returns.

2. **Debt Funds: Tax Treatment of Capital Gains**

   Debt funds invest in fixed-income securities like government bonds, corporate bonds, and money market instruments. The taxation of debt funds is more complex due to different treatments for short-term and long-term holdings:

   - **Short-Term Capital Gains (STCG) Tax on Debt Funds:**

   - If debt fund units are sold within **3 years** of investment, the profits are considered **short-term capital gains (STCG)**.
   - **Tax Rate:** STCG on debt funds is taxed according to the individual's **income tax slab**. This means the tax rate will depend on your overall taxable income, which could fall into the 20% or 30% tax bracket.

   Example:

   - You invest ₹1 lakh in a debt mutual fund and sell it after **2 years** for ₹1.05 lakh, making a gain of ₹5,000.
   - If you are in the **30% tax bracket**, the STCG tax on ₹5,000 would be **₹1,500**.
   - Your effective post-tax gain would be **₹3,500** (₹5,000 - ₹1,500).

   - **Long-Term Capital Gains (LTCG) Tax on Debt Funds:**

- If debt fund units are sold after **3 years**, the profits are considered **long-term capital gains (LTCG).**
- **Tax Rate:** LTCG on debt funds is taxed at **20%**, but with the **benefit of indexation**. Indexation adjusts the cost of acquisition to account for inflation, which reduces the capital gains on which tax is calculated.

Example:

- Suppose you invest ₹1 lakh in a debt mutual fund and sell it after **4 years** for ₹1.2 lakh, making a gain of ₹20,000.
- With **indexation**, your cost of acquisition is adjusted for inflation. If indexation increases your adjusted cost to **₹1.05 lakh**, the capital gain would be ₹15,000.
- The LTCG tax would then be **20% of ₹15,000**, which is **₹3,000**.
- Your post-tax profit would be **₹17,000** (₹20,000 - ₹3,000).

Understanding the tax treatment of debt funds is crucial for making informed decisions, especially if you are looking to maximize your post-tax returns. Indexation in long-term holdings can significantly reduce the capital gains, thus providing tax efficiency for long-term investors.

B. Strategies for Tax-Efficient Investing in Mutual Funds

To make the most of your mutual fund investments and minimize your tax liabilities, here are some strategies you can follow:

1. **Equity Funds:**
   - **Invest for the Long Term:**
   - The primary strategy for tax-efficient investing in equity funds is to hold your investments for more than **1 year**. By doing so, you can benefit from the **lower LTCG tax rate of 10%** on gains above ₹1 lakh. Long-term holding not only offers tax advantages but also helps you benefit from the potential for higher returns over time.
   - **Example:** If you invest ₹1 lakh in an equity fund and hold it for 3 years, you will only be subject to LTCG tax on any gains above ₹1 lakh, instead of paying 15% STCG tax if you had sold it within a year.
   - **Tax-Loss Harvesting:**
   - Tax-loss harvesting is a strategy where you sell investments that have incurred a loss to offset gains from other investments. If you have made profits in some funds, you can sell those where you have losses to reduce your taxable capital gains.
2. **Debt Funds:**
   - **Hold Debt Funds for More Than 3 Years:**
   - To take advantage of the **lower LTCG tax rate of 20%** with indexation, it's beneficial to hold debt funds for more than **3 years**. By doing so, you reduce the tax burden and benefit from the inflation-adjusted cost of acquisition, which lowers your taxable gains.
   - **Example:** If you invest in debt funds and hold them for 3 years or more, the 20% LTCG tax with

indexation could be significantly lower than if you sold them before 3 years, when STCG tax applies at your higher income tax rate.

- **Use Debt Funds in Your Tax-Advantaged Accounts:**
  - If possible, consider investing in debt funds through **tax-advantaged accounts** like the **Employee Provident Fund (EPF)** or **National Pension System (NPS)**, which provide tax deferral benefits.
  - **Example:** If you invest in a tax-deferred account like NPS, you will not pay taxes on the returns until you withdraw the funds at retirement, allowing you to benefit from compounding over the long term without worrying about annual taxes.

6. Risk and Return in Mutual Funds

When investing in mutual funds, understanding the relationship between risk and return is crucial. Each type of mutual fund comes with its own set of risks and potential returns. It's essential for investors to choose a fund that aligns with their financial goals, risk tolerance, and investment horizon.

A. Understanding the Risk Profile of Different Mutual Funds

Every mutual fund has a risk and return profile that is directly influenced by the underlying assets it invests in. These assets can range from high-risk equities to low-risk debt instruments. Below is a breakdown of the risk profiles of different types of mutual funds.

1. **Equity Funds: High-Risk, High-Return Potential**

   Equity funds primarily invest in stocks or shares of companies, offering high-return potential but also carrying a **high level of risk**. The value of these funds can fluctuate significantly due to the volatility in the stock market, driven by factors such as company performance, market sentiment, economic conditions, and global events.

   - **Risk Profile of Equity Funds:**

   ➢ **Market Risk:** The value of equity funds is directly affected by stock market performance. If the market goes up, the value of the fund typically rises, and vice versa.

   ➢ **High Volatility:** Equity funds are inherently volatile, meaning their value can change drastically in the short term. This volatility is influenced by both domestic and global factors.

   ➢ **Long-Term Growth Potential:** Despite the volatility, equities have historically outperformed other asset classes over the long term (e.g., bonds, real estate). Therefore, equity funds are suitable for long-term investors who can endure short-term fluctuations for potential high returns.

   ➢ **Risk Tolerance:** If you have a higher risk tolerance and a **long-term investment horizon** (5-10 years or more), equity funds can be a suitable investment. They allow you to weather short-term volatility and benefit from the overall growth of the economy and companies.

2. **Debt Funds: Low-Risk, Lower-Return**

   Debt funds invest in fixed-income securities, such as government bonds, corporate bonds, and money market instruments. These funds are typically **low-risk** and **less sensitive** to market fluctuations compared to **equity funds**. However, the risk in debt funds is primarily associated with factors like **interest rates**, **credit risk**, and **inflation risk**.

   Risk Profile of Debt Funds:

   - **Credit Risk:** Debt funds are exposed to the possibility that the bond issuer may default on its payments. This could happen if the issuer is unable to repay the principal or interest. This risk is higher for corporate bonds compared to government bonds.
   - **Interest Rate Risk:** When **interest rates** rise, the value of debt securities typically falls. This is because newer bonds offer higher interest rates, making older bonds with lower rates less attractive, which could lead to a decline in their market value.
   - **Inflation Risk:** Inflation can erode the real return on debt funds, particularly for longer-duration bonds.
   - **Stability and Regular Income:** Debt funds are suitable for more **conservative investors** who seek stability and a predictable stream of income, such as retirees or those with a short-to-medium investment horizon (1-5 years).

Return Potential:

- Debt funds generally offer **lower returns** than equity funds but are more **predictable** and **less volatile**.
- These funds focus on **capital preservation** and may provide regular income through interest payments, making them an attractive choice for investors looking for lower-risk options.

Example:

- If you invest ₹1 lakh in a **debt mutual fund** that primarily holds **government bonds**, the risk of losing money is low since government bonds are backed by the government.
- However, the **returns** will typically be modest compared to equity funds, and your investment will grow at a slower pace.
- Debt funds are ideal for investors who prioritize **capital preservation** over **aggressive growth**

3. **Hybrid Funds: A Mix of Both, Balancing Risk and Return**

Hybrid funds, also known as **balanced funds**, invest in a combination of equities and fixed-income securities (debt). The idea behind hybrid funds is to provide a balance between risk and return by investing in both higher-risk, higher-return assets like stocks, and lower-risk, lower-return assets like bonds.

- **Risk Profile of Hybrid Funds**:
    - Hybrid funds offer a **balanced approach** to risk. While they are not as volatile as pure equity funds,

they offer better growth potential than pure debt funds.

- These funds are ideal for investors who want some **equity exposure** for higher returns but also seek the **stability** provided by debt investments.
- The risk level of hybrid funds can vary based on their asset allocation. For instance, an aggressive hybrid fund may have a higher allocation to equities (e.g., 70% equity and 30% debt), whereas a conservative hybrid fund may have a higher allocation to debt (e.g., 30% equity and 70% debt).

➢ **Example**: If you invest ₹1 lakh in a hybrid fund that holds 60% equity and 40% bonds, the value of your investment will fluctuate based on the performance of both asset classes. If the stock market performs well, your equity portion will grow, but if interest rates rise and affect the bond market, your debt portion may provide a cushion. Hybrid funds can provide a balance of both **growth** and **stability**, making them suitable for **moderate-risk investors**.

B. Historical Return Data and How to Evaluate Fund Performance

While choosing a mutual fund, it's important to consider the **historical returns** as part of your decision-making process. However, it's crucial to understand that **past performance** is not always indicative of future results. That being said, historical performance can offer valuable insights into how the fund has performed under different market conditions.

1. **Evaluating Fund Performance Based on Historical Returns**

   When assessing the performance of a mutual fund, it's essential to consider several factors that provide insight into how well the fund has managed returns and risk over time. The key metrics include:

   ○ **1-Year, 3-Year, and 5-Year Returns:**

   ➢ **Short-Term Returns (1 Year):** These returns reflect how the fund has performed over a short period, and can be heavily influenced by market volatility. It's important to recognize that short-term returns may not be indicative of the fund's true potential.

   ○ **Example:** Suppose you are evaluating an equity fund that has delivered a **15% return over the past 5 years**. This figure gives a sense of the long-term performance. However, it's important to compare this with the fund's performance in the past 1 and 3 years as well, as those can be affected by recent market conditions.

   ➢ **Medium-to-Long-Term Returns (3 to 5 Years):** These returns offer a clearer picture of how the fund has navigated through various market conditions. Over the medium to long term, funds are likely to be exposed to different market cycles, allowing you to assess their ability to perform under varying conditions.

- **Comparison with Benchmark Index:**
- ➢ **Benchmark Comparison:** One of the most effective ways to evaluate a fund's performance is by comparing it to a relevant **benchmark index** (e.g., **Nifty 50** for equity funds or the **CRISIL Composite Bond Index** for debt funds). A **fund that consistently outperforms its benchmark** indicates strong management and an effective investment strategy.
- **Example:** If you are considering an equity fund that has returned **15%** over 5 years and its benchmark index (e.g., Nifty 50) has only returned **10%** over the same period, this suggests that the fund has been performing better than the market, which may be a positive sign.
- **Consistency in Performance:**
- ➢ **Consistency During Market Cycles:** It's essential to evaluate how consistently the fund performs, especially during periods of **market volatility** or downturns. Funds that can generate **positive returns** during market corrections or crashes are often more resilient and are better managed.
- **Example:** Consider a **debt fund** that has consistently delivered **7% returns** over the last 5 years, while fixed deposits (FDs) have only yielded **6%**. In this case, the debt fund has not only outperformed the FD but has done so consistently over the medium term, which can be appealing to conservative investors seeking stability.

Summary:

- **Performance Evaluation** should be based on **multiple time frames** (1-year, 3-year, and 5-year returns) to assess how the fund has managed to perform under different market conditions.
- Always compare the fund with an appropriate **benchmark index** to measure its relative performance.
- **Consistency** is key—funds that perform well even in market downturns tend to demonstrate better management and strategy, providing more **reliable** long-term returns.

2. **Understanding Volatility and Risk-Adjusted Returns**

When evaluating a mutual fund's performance, it's essential to look not only at the returns but also at the **volatility** and **risk-adjusted returns**. These metrics provide deeper insights into the consistency and stability of the fund's performance relative to the risk taken.

- **Volatility:**
- **Volatility** refers to the extent to which a fund's returns fluctuate over time. High volatility means that the returns can change significantly in a short period, while low volatility indicates more stable returns.
- **High Volatility:**
- Funds with high volatility typically have **greater potential for higher returns** but come with increased risk. These funds are more sensitive to

market fluctuations, which can lead to sharp ups and downs in performance.

- **Example:** An equity fund that invests in small-cap or emerging-market stocks tends to be more volatile because these markets are often subject to higher uncertainty, but they may offer higher returns in the long term.

- **Low Volatility:**

- Funds with low volatility may offer **stable returns** but with less potential for significant growth. These funds tend to be more conservative, often investing in more stable assets such as government bonds or large-cap stocks.
- **Example:** A debt fund investing in government bonds or blue-chip corporate bonds is likely to have lower volatility because the risk of default is lower, and the returns are more predictable.

- **Risk-Adjusted Return:**

- **Risk-adjusted return** is a measure of how much return a fund delivers for each unit of risk taken. It helps you understand whether a fund is providing adequate returns given the level of risk involved. Common tools to evaluate risk-adjusted return include the **Sharpe ratio** and **Sortino ratio**.

- **Sharpe Ratio:**

- The **Sharpe ratio** measures the excess return per unit of risk (volatility). A higher Sharpe ratio indicates that the fund is providing a higher return for the level of risk it's taking.

- **Formula:** Sharpe Ratio = (Return of the Fund - Risk-Free Rate) / Standard Deviation of the Fund's Returns
- **Example:** Fund A might offer a 10% return but with high volatility (risk), while Fund B offers an 8% return with lower volatility. If Fund A's Sharpe ratio is lower than Fund B's, it means that Fund B provides better risk-adjusted returns despite offering slightly lower returns.

- **Sortino Ratio:**

- The **Sortino ratio** is similar to the Sharpe ratio but focuses only on the downside risk, i.e., the risk of negative returns. It measures how much return a fund provides for every unit of downside risk.
- **Formula:** Sortino Ratio = (Return of the Fund - Risk-Free Rate) / Downside Deviation
- The Sortino ratio is useful for investors who are more concerned about losses rather than overall volatility.

Example of Risk-Adjusted Returns:

Suppose **Fund A** delivers **10% returns** but has high volatility (standard deviation), while **Fund B** delivers **8% returns** but with lower volatility. Upon calculating their Sharpe ratios:

- **Fund A** might have a Sharpe ratio of **0.5**.
- **Fund B** might have a Sharpe ratio of **0.8**.

In this case, **Fund B** is offering better **risk-adjusted returns** because it delivers nearly the same returns as Fund A but with lower risk.

3. **How to Use Historical Performance Data for Future Decisions**

   While historical performance data can provide valuable insights into how a fund has performed over time, it should not be the sole factor in making investment decisions. There are several key points to keep in mind when using historical performance for future investment decisions.

   - **Consider Current Market Conditions:**
   - ➢ **Market Cycle Impact:**
   - Historical returns are often influenced by the market cycle (bullish or bearish). If a fund performed exceptionally well during a market boom, it's important to evaluate whether such conditions are likely to persist or if a market correction is on the horizon.
   - **Example:** If you're looking at an equity fund that performed well in the past five years, and the market is currently in a bullish phase, the strong returns may have been boosted by the overall market conditions. In such a case, future performance may not mirror the past, especially if the market transitions to a bearish or volatile phase.
   - **Fund Manager's Strategy:**
   - ➢ A fund's past performance reflects the strategy of the fund manager, and it's important to assess whether

the manager's strategy is still aligned with the market environment. If the manager changes strategy or if there are structural changes within the fund (e.g., changes in the team or investment philosophy), past performance may not be indicative of future returns.

- **Example:** A fund may have historically focused on growth stocks, but if the manager shifts focus towards value stocks in the current market, the performance might differ from the historical pattern.
- **Industry and Economic Trends:**

➢ Changes in industry or economic conditions can significantly impact future returns. For example, sectors like technology, healthcare, or energy may perform differently based on economic trends, regulatory changes, or technological advancements.

- **Example:** If you're considering a fund that invests heavily in the technology sector, it's essential to consider the current state of the tech industry. If the industry is going through a phase of rapid growth, past performance may be reflective of current conditions. However, if the sector is facing regulatory challenges or slower growth, future performance may not align with historical trends.
- **Adjust Expectations for the Future:**

➢ Always adjust your expectations based on the future outlook, rather than relying entirely on historical returns. Look for economic indicators, market forecasts, and fund manager commentary to help guide your expectations for the fund's future performance.

- **Example:** If you're investing in an equity fund with a historical average return of 12% annually, but economic conditions suggest slower growth or potential downturns, adjust your expected returns accordingly. You should also be aware of factors that could lead to higher or lower returns, such as inflation, interest rates, and geopolitical risks.

7. **How to Monitor and Review Mutual Fund Investments**
Investing in mutual funds is not a one-time activity. Regular monitoring and periodic reviews are essential to ensure that your investments remain aligned with your financial goals and that you're on track for achieving them. Mutual fund performance can fluctuate due to various factors, such as market conditions, the fund manager's decisions, and shifts in economic cycles. Below is an in-depth guide on how to effectively monitor and review your mutual fund investments.

A. Tools and Platforms for Tracking Mutual Fund Performance

Several tools and platforms are available to help investors track their mutual fund investments efficiently. These platforms offer insights into the performance of funds, their Net Asset Value (NAV), portfolio holdings, historical returns, and other crucial metrics. By regularly using these tools, investors can stay informed about the status of their investments and make adjustments when necessary.

1. **Moneycontrol**

   Moneycontrol is one of the most popular financial websites in India for tracking mutual fund performance. It offers a comprehensive range of features that can help investors track their investments, including:

2. **Value Research Online**

   Value Research Online is another excellent platform for monitoring mutual fund investments. It is widely respected for its detailed analysis and reports on Indian mutual funds. Some of its key features include:

3. **ET Money**

4. **Other Platforms**

   Other than these major platforms, investors can also use apps like Groww, Zerodha, and Coin by Zerodha to track mutual fund performance. Each of these apps has its own set of features, such as detailed NAV data, return analysis, and the ability to monitor SIP investments.

B. The Importance of Reviewing Your Investments Periodically

Once you've invested in mutual funds, it's essential to conduct periodic reviews to ensure your investments remain in line with your financial goals. Life circumstances, market conditions, and even fund performance may change, so it's crucial to make adjustments when necessary. Below are several key reasons why reviewing your mutual fund investments periodically is important.

1. **Changes in Financial Goals**

   As your life progresses, your financial goals may evolve. A job promotion, marriage, the birth of a child, or approaching retirement can all lead to changes in how you should manage your investments.

   - **Example**: If you initially invested in equity funds because you were saving for a long-term goal (such as retirement in 15–20 years), but now you're saving for a down payment on a house in the next 5 years, you may need to reduce your exposure to high-risk equity funds and move some money into more stable debt funds.

2. **Changes in Risk Tolerance**

   Risk tolerance can fluctuate based on personal experiences, economic conditions, or market performance. For instance, if you're nearing retirement or have had negative experiences with market volatility, you may prefer to shift some of your equity investments to debt funds to reduce risk.

   - **Example**: If you invested heavily in equity mutual funds when you were younger, but now that you're nearing retirement, you might prefer the stability of debt funds to avoid market fluctuations as you approach your retirement date.

3. **Underperforming Funds**

   It's important to regularly check whether your mutual funds are performing well compared to their benchmarks. If a fund consistently underperforms its benchmark and peer funds, it may indicate poor fund management or a shift in its strategy. This is when you should consider reallocating your investments.

Example: Suppose you invested in an equity fund and expected it to outperform the Nifty 50 index over the long term. However, after 3 years, the fund has consistently lagged behind the Nifty index, and its risk-adjusted returns are below average. In this case, you may want to review the reasons for the underperformance and potentially switch to a better-performing fund.

4. **Fund Manager Changes**

   A mutual fund's performance is often closely tied to its fund manager. If the fund manager who has been managing the portfolio for several years leaves or is replaced, it may lead to a change in the fund's investment approach, risk profile, or returns. Monitoring the situation is essential to decide whether you want to stay invested in that fund.

   - **Example**: If a fund manager who has historically done well with their investment decisions leaves, the new fund manager may adopt a different strategy. This could impact the risk and return profile of the fund, prompting a review of whether the fund still meets your investment goals.

5. **Changes in Market Conditions**

   Market conditions can have a significant impact on mutual fund performance. Factors such as inflation, interest rates, political stability, and global economic changes can affect different asset classes in your portfolio. For example, when interest rates rise, bond prices fall, which can negatively affect debt funds.

Example: If you have invested in debt funds, and interest rates are rising, you might find that the value of your investments is declining. In such cases, it could be beneficial to switch to shorter-duration debt funds or even reconsider your investment in bonds altogether.

6. **Rebalancing the Portfolio**

   As your mutual fund investments grow, the proportion of different asset classes in your portfolio can shift due to different returns on equity and debt funds. For instance, your equity funds may perform well over time, causing their weight in the portfolio to rise. This could lead to an overexposure to equities, which might increase your risk beyond what you are comfortable with.

   - **Example**: If you started with a 60% equity and 40% debt allocation, but after a few years, the equity portion has grown to 75%, you may want to rebalance your portfolio by selling some equity funds and buying debt funds to bring the portfolio back to your preferred allocation.

Final Conclusion on this chapter

Understanding mutual funds is key to making informed investment decisions. By choosing the right fund based on your risk tolerance, investment goals, and timeline, you can build a diversified, well-managed portfolio. Whether you choose SIPs for steady growth or lump-sum investments for larger amounts, understanding taxation, risk, and return, as well as regularly

5

Real Estate Investment in India: Building Wealth through Property

Real estate is one of the most reliable ways to build wealth in India. Here's why it is so popular and how this chapter will help you understand it better:

1. **Potential for Growth:** Property values tend to increase over time, offering the chance for significant profits when sold (called capital appreciation).
2. **Steady Rental Income:** Owning property can provide a regular source of income through rent, making it a stable investment option.
3. **Tangible Asset:** Unlike stocks or mutual funds, real estate is something you can see, use, and even live in if needed.
4. **Focus of This Chapter:**
   - Explains different opportunities in real estate (residential, commercial, REITs).
   - Discusses challenges, like high costs or market risks.
   - Shares practical strategies for maximizing returns on your property investments.

This chapter will guide you to make smarter, more profitable real estate decisions in India!

1. **Residential vs. Commercial Investment**

   Residential Properties Investing in residential properties is often the first step for new investors due to:

   - **Ease of Understanding:** Most people are familiar with housing needs.
   - **Steady Demand:** Urbanization and nuclear families drive consistent demand.

   Example: Purchasing a 2BHK flat in a growing suburb like Noida or Pune can yield both rental income and long-term appreciation.

   Challenges: High upfront costs and lower rental yields (typically 2–4%).

   Commercial Properties Ideal for seasoned investors seeking higher rental yields (6–10%). This includes office spaces, retail shops, and warehouses.

   - **Advantages:** Long-term leases, higher cash flow.
   - **Risks:** Economic downturns can impact occupancy rates.

"Don't work for money; make it work for you."

—Robert T. Kiyosaki

2. **Rental Yields and Maximizing Value**

   Understanding Rental Yield

   Rental yield is a crucial metric in real estate investment. It helps determine the annual return you earn from your property as a percentage of its current market value. A higher rental yield indicates better profitability from the investment.

The **formula** to calculate rental yield is as follows:

Rental Yield (%) = (Annual Rental Income ÷ Property Value) × 100

Where:

- **Annual Rental Income** = Total rent received from the property over a year.
- **Property Value** = The current market price or purchase price of the property.

Example of Rental Yield Calculation

Suppose you own a property valued at ₹50,00,000 and earn ₹2,40,000 annually in rent.

Using the formula:

Rental Yield = (₹2,40,000 ÷ ₹50,00,000) × 100 = 4.8%

This means you earn a 4.8% return annually on your property's market value.

Strategies to Increase Rental Yields

1. **Choose Properties in Areas with Strong Infrastructure Growth**
   - Look for localities with upcoming metro stations, IT hubs, or highways.
   - These areas tend to attract tenants willing to pay higher rents.

   Example: Investing in properties near Hyderabad's HITEC City often results in higher rental yields due to demand from IT professionals.
2. **Invest in Interior Upgrades to Attract Premium Tenants**
   - Furnish the property with modern amenities like modular kitchens, air conditioning, and premium fittings.

- Well-maintained and aesthetically pleasing properties command higher rents.

Example: A fully furnished 2BHK apartment in Bengaluru's Whitefield area can fetch a 20–30% higher rental income compared to an unfurnished one.

3. **Leverage Online Platforms for Visibility**
   - Platforms like MagicBricks, 99acres, or NoBroker allow you to reach a larger pool of potential tenants.
   - Highlight features like proximity to schools, malls, and offices in your listing.

Example: Listing your property with high-quality photos and a detailed description can attract better tenants and even multiple offers.

> *"Good debt helps you grow; bad debt puts you in trouble. Use real estate as a tool for good debt."*
>
> —Robert T. Kiyosaki

3. **Understanding REITs (Real Estate Investment Trusts)**

What Are REITs?

A Real Estate Investment Trust (REIT) is a company that owns, operates, or finances income-generating real estate across various sectors such as commercial, residential, or industrial properties. It allows individual investors to pool their money into a diversified portfolio of real estate assets, much like mutual funds for stocks.

With REITs, you can earn returns from real estate without having to directly buy, manage, or maintain a property.

Benefits of Investing in REITs

1. **Liquidity:** Unlike physical property, REITs are traded on stock exchanges, making it easy to buy and sell.
2. **Professional Management:** The properties in a REIT are managed by professionals, ensuring maintenance and value optimization.
3. **Lower Entry Barriers:** REITs allow you to invest in real estate with small amounts of capital, unlike direct ownership, which requires significant upfront investment.
4. **Diversification:** By investing in a single REIT, you gain exposure to multiple properties across locations and sectors.

Examples of REITs in India

- **Embassy Office Parks REIT:** India's first listed REIT, primarily focused on office spaces in top cities like Bengaluru, Mumbai, and Pune.
- **Mindspace Business Parks REIT:** Focuses on commercial properties catering to technology hubs and business districts.

Both have provided steady income through dividends and appreciation in stock value.

Comparison to Direct Property Ownership

1. **Control:**
   - **REITs:** Limited control, as the management team handles property decisions.
   - **Direct Ownership:** Full control over the property but requires effort in management and maintenance.

2. **Risk:**
    - **REITs:** Spread across multiple properties, reducing the impact of a single underperforming asset.
    - **Direct Ownership:** Higher risk due to dependency on the performance of one property.
3. **Income:**
    - **REITs:** Regular dividends paid from rental income generated by the portfolio.
    - **Direct Ownership:** Income depends on renting out the property and timely rent payments.
4. **Cost:**
    - **REITs:** Entry is possible with a small investment, making it accessible for retail investors.
    - **Direct Ownership:** Requires a significant upfront investment for purchase and registration.

Who Should Invest in REITs?

REITs are ideal for:

- Individuals seeking **passive income** without the hassles of property management.
- Investors looking for **diversification** across real estate sectors.
- Those with a lower capital base but a desire to invest in real estate.

"Compound interest works not just in savings but also in real estate investments when rents and values grow over time."

—Morgan Housel

4. **Government Initiatives in Real Estate**

   1. **RERA (Real Estate Regulation and Development Act):**
      - Ensures transparency and accountability in property transactions.
      - Protects buyers from project delays and fraud.

   Impact: Increased trust among homebuyers, leading to better market stability.

   2. **Pradhan Mantri Awas Yojana (PMAY):**
      - Aims to provide affordable housing for all.
      - Offers subsidies to eligible buyers under the Credit Linked Subsidy Scheme (CLSS).

   Example: A first-time buyer in Tier-II cities like Lucknow or Indore can benefit from PMAY to reduce loan burdens.

"Success is not in what you have, but in who you are."

—Shiv Khera

5. **Tips for Long-term Success**

   Real estate investment, like any wealth-building strategy, requires careful planning, disciplined execution, and a focus on long-term goals. Below are some actionable tips to ensure sustainable success in this field:

1. **Location Matters**

   The location of your investment property is one of the most critical factors influencing its value and income potential.

- **Connectivity:** Properties near metro stations, highways, or airports typically see higher appreciation and demand.
- **Amenities:** Proximity to schools, hospitals, malls, and entertainment hubs makes a property attractive to families and professionals.
- **Job Markets:** Areas with thriving business districts or IT hubs attract tenants willing to pay premium rents.

Example: Investing in Navi Mumbai, which has excellent connectivity to Mumbai and is near the upcoming international airport, could yield substantial long-term benefits.

2. **Research Market Trends**

Before investing, analyze the current and future growth potential of an area. Look for infrastructure projects, government initiatives, or corporate expansions that could drive demand.

- **Local Demand:** Evaluate the property types in demand—luxury apartments, affordable housing, or commercial spaces.

Example: Properties in Bangalore's Sarjapur Road have seen exponential growth due to the establishment of IT parks and proposed metro lines.

3. **Leverage Debt Wisely**

While loans can amplify your buying power, they must be used strategically:

- **Opt for Cash Flow Positive Investments:** Choose properties where rental income exceeds EMI payments.
- **Avoid Over-leveraging:** Keep debt-to-income ratio manageable to avoid financial strain during downturns.
- **Take Advantage of Tax Benefits:** In India, home loans offer deductions under sections 80C and 24(b), reducing taxable income.

4. **Stay Patient and Think Long-term**

   Real estate is not a get-rich-quick scheme. Patience and a long-term perspective are vital for maximizing returns.

"Think big, but start small. Build your foundation strong, and the skyscraper of success will stand tall."

— Napoleon Hill

By focusing on these pillars, you can build a robust and profitable real estate portfolio. Remember, informed decisions today will lay the foundation for wealth and financial freedom tomorrow.

"Invest for the long term. The magic of compounding works best with time."

—Morgan Housel

6

Beyond Fixed Deposits: Modern Investment Strategies for Indian Families

For decades, Indian families have relied on **Fixed Deposits (FDs)** for their savings due to safety and guaranteed returns. However, with inflation often eroding real returns and modern options offering better growth, it's time to explore smarter investment strategies. Here's a breakdown:

Why Look Beyond Fixed Deposits?

Fixed Deposits (FDs) have been a go-to investment for Indian families because of their safety and guaranteed returns. However, changing financial landscapes and inflation make it essential to consider alternatives. Here's why:

1. **Low Returns**
   - FDs offer interest rates of around **5–7%**, which often struggle to keep up with inflation.
   - This means that the real value of your money (after adjusting for inflation) grows very little, if at all.

   Example: If inflation is 6% and your FD gives 5.5% interest, your purchasing power decreases over time.

2. **Tax Impact**
   - The interest earned on FDs is fully taxable as per your income slab.
   - For someone in the **30% tax bracket**, an FD offering 6% interest effectively gives just 4.2% post-tax.

   Example: On a ₹10 lakh FD earning ₹60,000 interest annually, ₹18,000 could go in taxes, leaving only ₹42,000 net income.
3. **Lack of Growth Potential**
   - FDs are designed for safety, not growth. They don't benefit from **compounding** or market-driven appreciation like other investments (e.g., equity or mutual funds).
   - Over time, this limits wealth creation.

"The rich don't work for money; they make money work for them."

—Robert T. Kiyosaki

Modern Investment Strategies

Moving beyond traditional investments like Fixed Deposits requires exploring modern strategies that offer better returns and greater flexibility. Here are two popular and effective approaches:

Systematic Investment Plans (SIPs) in Mutual Funds

- **What It Is:** SIPs allow you to invest a fixed amount of money regularly (e.g., monthly) in equity or debt mutual funds, making it easy to build wealth over time.

- **Advantages:**
  - **Potential for Higher Returns:** Equity mutual funds, particularly large-cap or index funds, have historically offered returns between **10–12% per year**, significantly outpacing FDs.
  - **Rupee Cost Averaging:** By investing consistently, you buy more units when prices are low and fewer when prices are high, reducing the impact of market volatility.

> *"The magic of compounding works best when you invest consistently."*
>
> —Morgan Housel

Stocks and ETFs (Exchange Traded Funds):

Investing in stocks and ETFs is a modern, flexible, and high-potential strategy to grow your wealth. Let's break it down:

What It Is

1. **Stocks:** Stocks represent ownership in a company. When you buy shares of a company, you become a partial owner and share in its profits and growth.
   - Stocks of well-established companies (like TCS, Reliance, or Infosys) are generally considered safer investments, while stocks of smaller, emerging companies may offer higher growth potential but come with more risk.
2. **ETFs (Exchange Traded Funds):** ETFs are a collection of stocks (or other securities) bundled into a single

product. They are traded on stock exchanges like individual stocks.

- **Index ETFs:** These track major indices such as **Nifty 50** or **Sensex**, giving exposure to the top-performing companies in India.
- **Sector ETFs:** These focus on specific industries like IT, banking, or energy.

Advantages

1. **High Growth Potential (Stocks):**
   - Over the long term, well-chosen stocks can deliver returns far exceeding traditional investments like FDs.
   - For example, stocks of companies like **TCS** or **HDFC Bank** have grown significantly as these companies expanded and generated higher profits.
   - Historically, the Indian stock market (e.g., Nifty 50) has delivered average annualized returns of **12–15%** over the last two decades.

   Key Insight: Investing in stocks requires patience and a focus on long-term growth. Markets may fluctuate in the short term, but quality companies tend to grow in value over time.
2. **Diversification and Low Risk (ETFs):**
   - ETFs provide exposure to multiple stocks in a single product, reducing the risk of relying on the performance of a single company.
   - **Example:** A Nifty 50 ETF includes the top 50 companies across various sectors, spreading your

investment and mitigating the risk of any one company or sector underperforming.

Low-Cost Option: ETFs are cheaper than mutual funds as they don't have high management fees. This makes them an affordable way to gain market exposure.

How to Start Investing in Stocks and ETFs

1. **Open a Demat and Trading Account:**
   - Choose a trusted broker (e.g., Zerodha, Upstox, or ICICI Direct) to start investing.
2. **Research Before Investing:**
   - Study companies' financials, growth potential, and industry trends for stock investments.
   - For ETFs, focus on the index or sector they track.
3. **Start Small:**
   - Begin with a small amount, understand the market, and gradually increase your investments.
4. **Monitor Performance Regularly:**
   - Keep an eye on your stocks or ETFs to ensure they align with your financial goals.

Example Scenarios

1. **Stocks:**
   - You buy **10 shares of TCS** at ₹3,500 each, spending ₹35,000. Over five years, as TCS grows, the stock price rises to ₹6,000 per share. Your investment is now worth ₹60,000.
   - Bonus dividends are an added benefit, often distributed by profitable companies.

2. **ETFs:**
   - You invest ₹10,000 in a **Nifty 50 ETF** when the index is at 20,000 points. If the index grows to 40,000 points in the next decade, your investment doubles to ₹20,000.

Risks and How to Mitigate Them

1. **Stock-Specific Risks:**
   - A company's stock may underperform due to poor management, industry changes, or economic conditions.
   - **Mitigation:** Research thoroughly and diversify your stock portfolio across sectors.
2. **Market Risks:**
   - The overall stock market may face downturns due to factors like global economic crises.
   - **Mitigation:** Focus on long-term goals and avoid panic selling during market dips.
3. **Liquidity Risk (ETFs):**
   - Some ETFs may have low trading volumes, making it harder to sell quickly.
   - **Mitigation:** Stick to popular ETFs with high liquidity, like Nifty 50 or Sensex ETFs.

"Risk comes from not knowing what you're doing. Educate yourself before you invest."

—Warren Buffett

Real Estate Investment Trusts (REITs)

What It Is

- A **Real Estate Investment Trust (REIT)** allows individuals to invest in a diversified portfolio of income-generating real estate assets without owning physical property. Essentially, REITs pool money from multiple investors to buy, manage, and develop real estate projects, such as office buildings, shopping malls, or residential complexes, and then distribute the rental income as dividends.

Advantages

- **Regular Income through Dividends:**
  - REITs provide a consistent stream of income through dividends, which are typically paid out quarterly or annually. This is a great way for investors to earn passive income from real estate without having to manage properties themselves.
- **Low Entry Barriers Compared to Buying Property:**
  - Investing in physical real estate often requires a large upfront capital investment, and the process of buying, maintaining, and selling property can be complex. REITs, on the other hand, allow investors to start with relatively smaller amounts of money. This makes it more accessible for retail investors to gain exposure to the real estate sector.

- **Diversification:**
  - Since REITs typically invest in a portfolio of properties across various locations and sectors (residential, commercial, industrial), they offer built-in diversification. This helps reduce risk compared to investing in a single property.
- **Liquidity:**
  - REITs are traded on stock exchanges, meaning you can buy and sell them easily, providing liquidity that is often lacking in direct real estate investments. Unlike physical real estate, you don't need to wait for a buyer for months.

Example: Embassy Office Parks REIT

- **Embassy Office Parks REIT** is an example of a popular REIT in India. It provides exposure to a diversified portfolio of commercial office spaces in key business districts. Through this REIT, investors can gain access to high-quality office spaces without the need to directly purchase or manage property.
  - For instance, if you invested ₹1 lakh in Embassy Office Parks REIT, you could earn dividends from the rental income generated by these office spaces. This provides a relatively stable, passive income stream.

"The rich don't work for money; they make money work for them."

—**Robert T. Kiyosaki**

In conclusion, **REITs** offer a simple and efficient way to invest in real estate without the challenges of property ownership. They provide a reliable income stream, accessibility for small investors, and the potential for diversification and growth, making them an attractive option for anyone looking to invest in real estate without the high capital requirements.

Gold and Digital Gold: A Modern Approach to a Traditional Asset

Gold has always been a reliable and trusted investment, especially in India, where it holds cultural and financial significance. Modern investment options such as **Gold ETFs**, **Sovereign Gold Bonds (SGBs)**, and **Digital Gold** make investing in gold more convenient and accessible for everyone.

What It Is

- **Gold ETFs (Exchange Traded Funds):**
  - Gold ETFs are investment funds that track the price of gold. These funds are traded on the stock exchange like shares, meaning you don't own physical gold but benefit from the price movement of gold. They are a hassle-free way to invest in gold without the need for physical storage.
- **Sovereign Gold Bonds (SGBs):**
  - SGBs are issued by the Government of India and are a hybrid investment product. They allow you to invest in gold while earning a fixed annual interest (currently **2.5%**) in addition to the potential for gold

price appreciation. The bonds have an 8-year maturity period and are tax-free if held until maturity.

- **Digital Gold:**
  - Digital gold platforms (such as Paytm, PhonePe, and SafeGold) allow you to buy gold in small amounts, starting from as little as ₹1. This gold is stored in a digital form, and you can redeem it for physical gold or cash later. It's an easy way to own gold without dealing with storage or security issues.

Advantages

- **Hedge Against Inflation:**
  - Gold is often seen as a safe haven during inflationary periods. Unlike paper currencies, gold generally holds or increases its value when inflation rises, which makes it an ideal asset for wealth preservation.
- **Liquidity and Convenience:**
  - Gold ETFs and digital gold are very easy to trade compared to physical gold. You don't need to worry about finding a buyer or managing physical storage. These investments can be bought and sold quickly through online platforms.
- **Diversification:**
  - Including gold in your portfolio helps reduce overall risk, especially when other assets like stocks or bonds are volatile. Gold's value tends to move differently from other assets, making it a good tool for balancing your investment mix.

- **Additional Returns with Sovereign Gold Bonds:**
  - SGBs offer not just gold price appreciation but also **2.5% annual interest**, making them a more attractive option compared to regular gold investments. This interest is paid yearly, and since it is government-backed, the security is higher.

Example: Sovereign Gold Bonds

- Suppose you invest ₹50,000 in Sovereign Gold Bonds when the gold price is ₹5,000 per gram (for 10 grams). Over the 8-year period, the gold price appreciates, and you also earn annual interest.
  - Annual Interest: ₹50,000 × 2.5% = ₹1,250 (paid yearly)
  - Over 8 years, this interest adds up to ₹10,000 in addition to any increase in gold prices.
  - If the price of gold rises to ₹7,000 per gram by the time the bond matures, your principal investment grows to ₹70,000. This appreciation in gold price and interest earned is tax-free when held till maturity.

Comparison with Physical Gold Investing in digital gold, ETFs, or SGBs has several advantages over physical gold. While physical gold requires storage, insurance, and verification of purity, digital gold and ETFs eliminate these issues. You don't need to worry about storing it in a safe or dealing with the complications of reselling it.

- Additionally, SGBs provide a fixed interest return, which physical gold does not offer. When investing in gold ETFs or digital gold, you are also ensuring liquidity and ease of transaction without the need to physically handle or store the gold.

Points to Remember

- **Taxation:**
  - Capital gains on gold ETFs and digital gold are subject to taxation. If held for less than 3 years, they are taxed as short-term capital gains; if held for more than 3 years, they are taxed as long-term capital gains. However, **SGBs** are tax-free if held until maturity, making them a very attractive option. Number of years are subject to change in any financial year.
- **Market Timing:**
  - Gold prices can fluctuate based on various factors such as global economic conditions, currency values, and market sentiment. It's important to take a long-term view when investing in gold, as prices may not always rise in the short term.
- **Allocation:**
  - Gold should generally constitute **5–15%** of your overall portfolio, depending on your risk tolerance and investment goals. This ensures a balanced approach and helps in managing risk while still benefiting from gold's long-term value retention.

"Gold is timeless. It's a store of value that outlasts economies and currencies."

—Brian Tracy

By utilizing modern options like **Gold ETFs**, **Sovereign Gold Bonds**, and **Digital Gold**, you can access the benefits of gold investment without the complexities of owning physical gold. These methods provide convenience, security, and growth potential, making gold a valuable asset in your portfolio for achieving long-term financial goals.

Key Considerations Before Investing

Before you begin investing, it's important to evaluate several key factors to ensure your investment strategy aligns with your goals and risk appetite. Here are the key considerations to keep in mind:

1. **Understand Your Risk Tolerance**
   - ➢ **High-Risk, High-Reward Options:**
   - ○ Equity markets (stocks) and startup investments typically offer higher returns, but they also come with a higher level of risk. The value of these investments can fluctuate widely based on market conditions or the success of the company. If you have a higher tolerance for risk and can handle market volatility, these could be suitable options.
   - ➢ **Safer Alternatives:**
   - ○ If you prefer stability and lower risk, consider safer investment options like debt mutual funds or the **National Pension Scheme (NPS)**. These options generally offer more predictable returns and are less impacted by market volatility compared to equities. Debt funds invest in government bonds or corporate

debt, while the NPS is a government-backed pension scheme that invests in a mix of debt and equity.

2. **Set Clear Goals**
   - **Short-Term Goals (1-3 years):**
     - For goals you plan to achieve within 1-3 years, it's best to focus on liquid or short-term debt funds. These funds are designed to protect your principal while providing moderate returns, making them ideal for parking money you might need soon. Examples include **Liquid Funds** or **Short-Term Debt Funds**, which have lower risk but offer limited returns.
   - **Long-Term Goals (5+ years):**
     - For long-term goals (5 years or more), investments like **equity**, **gold**, or **real estate** are more appropriate. These assets tend to grow over time, although they come with higher short-term volatility. Equity investments, in particular, have historically outperformed other assets over the long run, and gold acts as a hedge against inflation.
3. **Stay Diversified**
   - **Spread Investments Across Asset Classes:**
     - Diversification is a key principle of sound investing. By spreading your investments across different asset classes (stocks, bonds, gold, real estate, etc.), you reduce the overall risk of your portfolio. For example, if one asset class (like stocks) performs poorly, other assets (like gold or bonds) may perform well, helping to balance the overall returns.

"Do not put all your eggs in one basket."

The Role of Financial Freedom

Financial freedom is more than just a buzzword; it's the ultimate goal for many investors. It signifies the ability to live life on your own terms, free from financial constraints, and with the peace of mind that comes from knowing your money is working for you. To achieve this, investing plays a crucial role. Through smart investment strategies, you can build wealth that generates passive income, enabling you to focus on what truly matters in life.

1. **Investing to Build Wealth**

   - **The Importance of Starting Early:**
     - The journey to financial freedom begins with the decision to invest. The earlier you start, the more you can benefit from the power of compounding. Compounding allows your investment returns to generate additional returns, which accelerates the growth of your wealth over time. This principle is especially impactful in equity markets, real estate, and other growth assets.
   - **Building Passive Income Streams:**
     - The ultimate aim of investing is to build passive income streams—income that requires little to no active involvement. These income sources might come from dividends, rental income, capital appreciation, or interest from fixed-income investments. Passive income provides financial security, as it continues to flow even if you stop working.

2. **Achieving Financial Independence**
   - **Replacing Active Income with Passive Income:**
     - Financial independence means having sufficient income from your investments to cover your living expenses. For example, if your monthly expenses are ₹50,000, and your investments generate ₹50,000 per month in passive income, you no longer need to rely on your job or active income.
   - **Real-World Example:**
     - Many people who achieve financial freedom do so by investing in dividend-paying stocks, rental properties, or business ventures that generate consistent income. This allows them to retire early, pursue a passion project, or even take time off to travel or spend time with family without worrying about money.
   - **Controlling Your Time:**
     - Financial freedom offers the most valuable asset—time. When you don't have to worry about working for money, you can focus on the things that truly matter to you. You can spend more time with loved ones, engage in hobbies, or dedicate yourself to causes that align with your values. Financial independence offers freedom of choice, enabling you to decide how you spend your days.
3. **Compound Growth and Wealth Accumulation**
   - **Power of Compounding:**
     - One of the most effective ways to build wealth is through compounding. Compounding refers to

the process where the returns you earn on your investments begin to generate their own returns. The longer you stay invested, the more powerful compounding becomes.

- **Growth Assets for Wealth Accumulation:**
  - Investing in growth assets like **equities**, **real estate**, and **mutual funds** is essential for long-term wealth accumulation. These asset classes generally offer higher returns than more conservative investments, such as **bonds** or **fixed deposits**. While growth assets may carry more risk, they also have the potential to generate much higher returns over time, which is crucial for achieving financial independence.

4. **Financial Freedom and Lifestyle Control**

- **Financial Freedom and Lifestyle Choices:**
  - Once you achieve financial freedom, the control over your lifestyle is immense. You no longer need to work for a paycheck or rely on a job that might not align with your personal goals or values. Instead, you can choose to work on projects you're passionate about, travel, volunteer, or even pursue entrepreneurship.
- **Example:**
  - Many people dream of retiring early and enjoying their life while still being young and healthy. Through smart investing, it's possible to accumulate enough wealth to support this lifestyle. For example,

investing in **real estate** for passive income or **SIPs** for long-term growth can help you retire early.

5. **Risk Management and Financial Freedom**
   - **Minimizing Risk:**
     - Financial freedom isn't just about accumulating wealth—it's also about managing risk. A well-diversified portfolio, consisting of various asset classes such as equities, real estate, bonds, and gold, helps reduce the risk of significant losses. The key is to balance higher-risk investments with safer, more stable assets.
   - **Quote for Thought:**

"Risk comes from not knowing what you're doing."

— **Warren Buffett**

- This emphasizes the importance of educating yourself before making any investment decisions. By understanding the risks involved and staying diversified, you can minimize potential setbacks and continue building wealth toward financial freedom.

"Success is not about working hard but working smart and making money work for you."

—**Shiv Khera**

7

The Power of Compounding: A Long-Term Investment Guide for Indian Investors

Understanding Compounding:

- **What is Compounding?**
  - Compounding refers to the process where the returns you earn on your investments start generating additional returns. Over time, your initial investment and the accumulated earnings both generate further earnings.
  - In simple terms, it means your money starts to "earn money." The returns from your investment are reinvested, creating a snowball effect where your wealth grows faster as time progresses.
- **Why is Compounding Important?**
  - The longer your money remains invested, the more it compounds, which accelerates wealth growth. It's often called "the eighth wonder of the world" because of its ability to multiply wealth exponentially over time.

- **Example:**
  - If you invest ₹1,00,000 at an annual return of 10%, after 1 year you will have ₹1,10,000. In the second year, you earn 10% not only on your original ₹1,00,000, but also on the ₹10,000 interest from the first year. As a result, your returns grow faster as time progresses.

> *"The most powerful force in the universe is compound interest."*
>
> **—Albert Einstein**

- **Impact of Time on Compounding:**
  - The effect of compounding is most noticeable when you give your investments time to grow. With the passage of time, the returns you earn keep building upon themselves, creating a much larger wealth base than initial investments alone would yield.
- **Example:**
  - If you invest ₹10,000 at an annual return of 12%, after 10 years, it would grow to ₹31,058. In contrast, if you had delayed investing for 5 years, you would have missed out on a significant portion of that growth.
  - The more time you allow, the more powerful compounding becomes. This is why starting early in life can yield exponential wealth over time.

By understanding the power of compounding, Indian investors can appreciate the importance of long-term, disciplined investing, which allows them to harness the full potential of their money and create substantial wealth for the future.

The Importance of Starting Early:

- ➢ **The Power of Compounding Over Time:**
- ○ Compounding is often called the "eighth wonder of the world" because of its ability to exponentially grow wealth over time. When you invest early, your money earns returns not only on your initial principal amount but also on the accumulated returns from previous periods. This process snowballs as time progresses.
- ○ The more time you give your investments to compound, the greater the final value of your wealth. Even modest initial investments can grow significantly over a long period, highlighting the importance of starting early.
- ➢ **Why Starting Early is Critical:**
- ○ **Time Is Your Best Friend:**
- ○ In investing, time is your most valuable asset. The longer you allow your investments to compound, the larger the impact. For example, if you start investing at age 25, your money will have 35 years to grow before you reach retirement at age 60. The same investment at age 35 only has 25 years to grow, reducing the power of compounding.
- ➢ **Small Contributions, Big Impact:**
- ○ Even if you start with small amounts, compounding can turn modest contributions into substantial sums

over time. The key is to stay consistent and allow the investment to grow.

- **Example of the Impact of Starting Early:**
    - **Scenario 1 (Starting at 25):**
    - Let's assume you invest ₹5,000 every month at a return of 12% per year. By the time you reach 60, you could have accumulated over ₹1 crore. Here's how it breaks down:
    - Monthly Investment: ₹5,000
    - Annual Return: 12%
    - Time: 35 years
    - Accumulated Amount: ₹1.02 crore
- **Scenario 2 (Starting at 30):**
    - Now, if you delay starting by just 5 years and start at age 30, your investment will have only 30 years to grow. The total amount accumulated will be much lower, around ₹68 lakh instead of ₹1 crore. This is a direct consequence of the compounding process not having enough time to work its magic.
    - **Key Takeaway:**
    - Starting 5 years earlier could mean a difference of ₹34 lakh, which illustrates how significant time is in maximizing the benefits of compounding.
- **The Importance of Early Action in Wealth Creation:**
    - The earlier you start, the less you need to invest to reach your financial goals. If you wait until later in life

to start investing, you will either need to invest larger amounts or accept a smaller corpus at retirement.

- **Delayed Gratification:**
  - Starting early requires a bit of discipline, as you may need to put aside money when other expenses seem more urgent. But this early investment allows you to take advantage of compounding, ultimately leading to greater wealth without requiring significant sacrifices later on.

"Don't wait to buy real estate. Buy real estate and wait."

—T. Harv Eker

- **Impact of Delaying Investments:**
  - **The Cost of Waiting:**
  - Delaying the start of investing has a clear cost: less time for your investment to grow. For instance, if you delay your investment by 10 years, you may have to contribute more money every month to catch up on the growth you missed out on. This delay in compounding can also significantly reduce the final value of your investments.
- **What Happens If You Delay by 5 or 10 Years?**
  - Starting at age 30 instead of 25 could cut the accumulated wealth by nearly 30%. Starting at 40 instead of 30 could result in even bigger losses. This highlights why the first few years of an investment journey are crucial to building long-term wealth.

- **The Exponential Growth of Investments Over Time:**
  - In the initial years, compounding might seem slow, but as time passes, the growth accelerates. A ₹1,000 investment might not seem much at first, but after 20 or 30 years of compounding, it can transform into a much larger sum.
- **Example:**
  - If you invest ₹10,000 every month at an annual return of 12% for 20 years, you could have over ₹2.5 crore. However, starting just 5 years later would mean reducing the total accumulated amount by ₹1 crore, showcasing the powerful effect of time.
- **Real-World Example:**
  - A well-known example of compounding in action is Warren Buffett, one of the world's richest investors. His net worth grew largely due to the compounded returns on his early investments. Buffett himself started investing at age 11, which allowed him to benefit from decades of compounding.

The Key to Successful Long-Term Investing:

- **Discipline and Consistency:**
  - The key to maximizing the power of compounding is disciplined, long-term investing. Regularly investing, even in small amounts, can create enormous wealth over time, so it's important to start as soon as possible.

- **Long-Term Vision:**
  - Compounding rewards those who think long-term. The earlier you start, the easier it becomes to reach financial independence. Even though the results may not be immediately visible, trust the process and allow time to work in your favor.

By starting early, you position yourself to benefit from compounding at its best. You can grow your wealth with less effort and fewer contributions, allowing your money to work for you, rather than you working for it

How Compounding Works Over Time – A Detailed Explanation

- **Understanding the Slow Start:**
  - When you first begin investing, the returns may seem modest, and the growth of your investment may feel slow. This is because in the early stages, the interest or returns are being calculated on the initial amount invested, which is still relatively small. However, as time progresses, the returns you've already earned begin to generate additional returns. This process is the essence of compounding.
  - Compounding means that your returns are reinvested to generate more returns. Over time, as the returns accumulate, they start to earn returns themselves, creating a snowball effect. In simple terms, it's like earning money on your money.

- **Example:**
  - **Initial Investment:** Imagine you start by investing ₹1,00,000 in a mutual fund that provides an annual return of 10%.
- **Year 1:**
  - You earn 10% of ₹1,00,000, which is ₹10,000.
  - After the first year, you now have ₹1,10,000 (₹1,00,000 + ₹10,000).
- **Year 2:**
  - In the second year, you earn 10% on ₹1,10,000, which is ₹11,000.
  - So, at the end of the second year, you have ₹1,21,000.
- **Year 3:**
  - In the third year, you earn 10% on ₹1,21,000, which is ₹12,100.
  - Now your total becomes ₹1,33,100.
  - The key point here is that in Year 1, your return was ₹10,000. In Year 2, your return was ₹11,000, and in Year 3, it was ₹12,100. As you can see, the returns are increasing each year, not because you are adding more money, but because you are earning interest on the interest.
- **The Exponential Growth of Compounding:**
  - While the returns might seem slow initially, compounding's true power becomes apparent over a longer period. The longer you leave your investment untouched, the more pronounced the growth becomes.

- **Example of 10 Years of Compounding:**
  - If you leave your ₹1,00,000 investment for 10 years at an annual return of 10%, you would have ₹2,59,374 at the end of 10 years. This is the power of compounding—returns on returns.
- **Example of 20 Years of Compounding:**
  - If you were to leave that same ₹1,00,000 invested for 20 years at the same rate of 10%, you would have ₹6,72,749 at the end of the period.
  - This demonstrates how compounding accelerates over time. As the time period extends, the returns multiply, and the growth becomes exponential.
- **How Compounding Works Best with Time:**
  - In the early years, your investment grows slowly because the amount you're earning on the original investment is small. But after several years, as the investment continues to grow, the amount earned on that growth becomes larger and larger, making the overall growth rate significantly higher.
- **The Power of Patience:** The reason compounding is often referred to as the "eighth wonder of the world" is because, over time, it can turn small investments into large sums. The earlier you start and the longer you stay invested, the more you can benefit from compounding.
- **The Magic of Consistency and Compounding:**
  - Compounding is not just about the length of time but also about consistency. If you consistently invest over

time, even small amounts, the power of compounding will work wonders. This is why it's important to start as early as possible and continue investing regularly, without trying to time the market or looking for short-term gains.

- **Example:**
  - Let's say you invest ₹5,000 every month in an equity mutual fund that gives an annual return of 12%. After 10 years, you could potentially accumulate ₹20 lakhs or more, assuming the same return.
  - By contributing regularly, even small amounts, you will benefit from both compounding on your initial investment and compounding on the returns you've earned from past contributions.
  - This shows the power of regular investing, even in small amounts, as it adds up over time.

"The magic of compounding works best when you invest consistently."

—**Morgan Housel**

- **The Compounding Formula (For Better Understanding):**
  - The formula to calculate compound interest is: $\mathbf{A = P(1 + r/n)^{(nt)}}$
  - A = the amount of money accumulated after n years, including interest.
  - P = principal amount (initial investment).
  - r = annual interest rate (decimal).

- n = number of times that interest is compounded per year.
- t = number of years the money is invested for.
- **Example:**
- If you invest ₹1,00,000 at 10% annual interest for 10 years, the formula would give you the total amount you'll have after 10 years, factoring in compounding.
- If interest is compounded yearly (n = 1), the formula becomes: **A = ₹1,00,000 * (1 + 0.10)^10 = ₹2,59,374**
- This formula shows how your initial investment grows exponentially over time due to compounding.

➢ **Why Consistent Investing Matters:**

- Every time you invest, your money not only earns returns on the original investment but also on the accumulated returns from previous periods. This cumulative effect is what accelerates the growth of your wealth over time.
- As Morgan Housel points out, compounding works best when you invest consistently. Over time, the growth of your money will shift from a linear path to an exponential one.

How Compounding Accelerates Over Time

➢ **Exponential Growth Over Time:**

- Compounding doesn't just add a fixed amount to your investment each year. Instead, it adds returns on the returns you've already earned, creating a snowball effect. This exponential growth means that the longer you stay invested, the faster your money grows.

- The first few years of investment might seem slow, but as time passes, the growth becomes significantly faster. In the initial years, your interest is small because it's only based on your principal amount. However, over time, your interest starts accumulating on both the principal and the previously earned interest, leading to exponential growth.

➢ **The Early Years Matter:**

- While compounding accelerates over time, it's essential to start early. Even if you invest a modest sum, the more years your money is compounding, the larger the eventual sum will be. Small, consistent contributions can lead to substantial wealth in the future.
- The earlier you start, the more your initial investments have time to compound, resulting in larger gains. Even if you don't have the ability to invest large amounts, investing early gives your money more time to grow.

➢ **Example of Compounding Impact:**

- Let's say you invest ₹1,000 every month in an equity mutual fund, and it earns an average return of 12% annually.
- In the first year, your ₹1,000 grows to ₹1,120 (assuming a 12% return), but the next year, your return is calculated not just on ₹1,000, but on ₹1,120 (the new amount).

- The growth starts accelerating as more of your returns start earning their own returns. After 20 years, you would have invested ₹2.4 lakh (₹1,000 each month for 20 years). But due to compounding, your total investment grows to over ₹14 lakh.
- This shows how your ₹1,000 contributions start working harder over time, not just earning returns on the principal but also on the accumulated interest.

The Importance of Patience in Compounding

- **The Slow Start vs. The Exponential Growth:**
  - Initially, the growth from compounding can feel slow, especially when you first start. But with each passing year, the growth begins to compound more rapidly, and what seemed like slow growth in the early years starts accelerating.
  - **First 5 years**: Your returns are based on your initial principal, and the growth is linear.
  - **After 10–15 years**: Now, the returns start compounding on the accumulated returns, making your wealth grow at a faster rate.
  - **After 20 years or more**: At this stage, compounding is working on a larger sum, and you may see your wealth skyrocket in a way that seems almost magical.
- **Why Patience is Key:**
  - As the old saying goes, "Rome wasn't built in a day." Similarly, wealth from compounding isn't created overnight. The longer you stay invested, the more powerful the effect of compounding becomes.

- The key is to stay invested and allow time to do its work. You don't need to make big, risky bets or take on too much risk. By investing consistently and for the long term, you let the power of compounding generate wealth on your behalf.

The Power of Time: "Time is Your Most Valuable Asset"

- **The Time Factor:**
  - Time is the most crucial component of the compounding process. The longer you leave your money invested, the more it can grow.
  - Even if you invest a small amount, if you start early, your investment will grow into a much larger sum by the time you retire, simply because of the compounding effect over the years.
- **Why Delaying Hurts:**
  - Every year you delay starting your investment is a year you lose the opportunity for your returns to compound. This can result in missed opportunities for wealth accumulation.
  - If you delay your investments for just a few years, you may find that you need to invest much more aggressively later to achieve the same results. For example, delaying a ₹1,000 monthly SIP by 5 years could mean losing out on significant compounded growth.
- **The Compound Growth Curve:**
  - Think of the growth curve as an upward curve that starts out slow and then steepens rapidly over time. In

the beginning, you might think, "Is this all?" But as time progresses, the curve becomes steeper, and the growth becomes substantial.

- The longer you allow your money to grow, the more pronounced this "steepening" becomes. For example, you may only see modest returns in the first few years, but in the later years, your returns grow disproportionately larger.

The Best Way to Harness Compounding

- **Consistency:**
  - The key to harnessing the full power of compounding is consistency. Make regular, fixed investments over time, and don't try to time the market. The more consistent you are, the more your returns will add up and compound over the years.
  - Whether you invest monthly through SIPs, or make annual lump-sum contributions, the regularity of your investments helps your money grow steadily.
- **Reinvestment:**
  - Reinvesting the returns you earn is another essential part of maximizing the power of compounding. When you take your dividends, interest, or capital gains and reinvest them, they start earning returns as well, creating a snowball effect.
  - If you invest in stocks or mutual funds, ensure that the dividends are reinvested into the same or other investments. This accelerates the process of growth.

The Role of Discipline in Long-Term Investing

Discipline is the cornerstone of successful long-term investing. It's not just about putting your money into investments but about staying consistent, adhering to a strategy, and having the patience to let your investments grow over time. The process of compounding—where the returns on your investments earn additional returns—relies heavily on time and consistency. Without discipline, this potential can be severely diminished.

The Power of Consistent Investment:

- **Consistency in Contribution:**
  - Discipline in investing means committing to a regular schedule. Whether it's monthly, quarterly, or annually, consistently investing allows your portfolio to grow over time.
  - The key point here is **automatic, scheduled investments**. For example, you set up an SIP (Systematic Investment Plan) for ₹5,000 every month and forget about it. You do this whether the markets are up or down, whether you feel optimistic or pessimistic. This approach means that you don't get swayed by market sentiment or daily fluctuations.
- **Why Consistency Matters:**
  - It's often easy to fall prey to the temptation to invest when markets are doing well and avoid investing when markets are low. But disciplined investors understand that investing regularly, regardless of the

market's mood, takes advantage of something called **rupee cost averaging**.

- ○ **Rupee cost averaging** means that when the market is down, your ₹5,000 buys more units of the asset at a cheaper price, and when the market is up, it buys fewer units. Over time, this helps you buy investments at an average price, smoothing out market volatility.

The Importance of Staying Committed:

- ➢ **Don't Let Short-Term Market Volatility Discourage You:**
- ○ Investing in stocks, mutual funds, or any volatile asset class requires the ability to withstand market fluctuations. Short-term drops in the value of your investments may cause doubt or anxiety, but this is where discipline plays a pivotal role. Staying the course during market corrections or dips enables you to benefit from long-term growth once the market rebounds.
- ➢ **Avoiding Panic and Emotion-Driven Decisions:**
- ○ The most common pitfall in investing is making emotional decisions based on fear or greed. When markets are volatile, it's natural to feel panic or to try and "time" the market (buying when things are cheap and selling when they're high). However, **timing the market is extremely difficult** and often leads to missed opportunities.

- By staying disciplined, you're removing emotional decision-making from your investments. You don't try to outguess the market—you trust the process.

The Ripple Effect of Small, Consistent Investments:

- **Even Small Contributions Matter:**
  - The power of small, consistent contributions cannot be overstated. Even if you start with a modest amount, like ₹5,000 per month, over a long period, those contributions build up significantly through compounding.
- **Compound Growth Over Time:**
  - Compounding accelerates growth as time passes. In the beginning, the returns might feel small, but the magic happens in the later years as the returns earned start generating more returns.
  - The earlier you start, the more time compounding has to work. For example, starting an SIP at age 25 rather than 35 gives an additional 10 years of compounding. This extra time can lead to vastly different outcomes.

Market Volatility: The Test of Discipline:

- Markets are inherently volatile. In the short term, asset values can fluctuate widely. However, in the long run, equity markets tend to grow. The discipline of staying invested through volatility is what helps you benefit from this growth.
- Imagine an investor who started in 2007, just before the global financial crisis. While the market crashed

in 2008, the investor stayed disciplined and continued investing regularly. By the time the market recovered in 2013 and beyond, the returns were substantial. This is why starting early and staying disciplined through market cycles is so important.

> *"The key to success is to focus on goals, not obstacles."*
>
> *—Brian Tracy*

The Impact of Discipline on Your Financial Journey:

- **The Compound Effect:**
  - When you consistently contribute to your investment account, even if you can only manage small amounts, the compound effect over time becomes significant. A disciplined investor who sticks to a strategy will see their wealth multiply in ways that non-disciplined investors won't.
- **Understanding that Long-Term Investing Is Not About Quick Wins:**
  - Long-term investing is about trusting the process. The rewards are not instant, and the path may not always be smooth. However, the consistent application of effort pays off in the long run.

Case Study: The Impact of Compounding in Equity Investments

Compounding is a powerful force that helps your investments grow exponentially over time. It's often referred to as "the eighth wonder of the world" because of its ability to turn small, consistent investments into significant wealth. In this case study, we will examine how compounding works in the context of equity investments, where stock prices and returns can compound over time.

Example 1: ₹1 Lakh Invested 10 Years Ago

- **Initial Investment:** ₹1,00,000 (₹1 lakh)
- **Annual Return (r):** 12%
- **Investment Period (t):** 10 years

Understanding the Formula for Compounding:

To calculate the future value of an investment based on compounding, we use the compound interest formula, which is:

Formula: A = P * (1 + r/100)^t

Where:

- **A** = The amount after the investment period (future value)
- **P** = Principal amount (the initial investment)
- **r** = Annual interest rate (in percentage)
- **t** = Time period (in years)

Substituting the Values:

Using the formula above, let's plug in the values for a ₹1 lakh investment at 12% annual return over 10 years.

A = 1,00,000 * (1 + 12/100)^10

A = 1,00,000 * (1.12)^10

A = 1,00,000 * 3.10585

A = ₹3,10,585

So, after 10 years, an initial investment of ₹1 lakh at an annual return of 12% grows to **₹3,10,585**.

Explanation of Growth:

- In the first year, the investment grows by ₹12,000 (12% of ₹1,00,000), bringing the total value to ₹1,12,000.
- In the second year, the 12% return is now applied to ₹1,12,000, which means the growth for the second year is ₹13,440, making the total value ₹1,25,440.
- Over time, as the amount grows, the returns themselves start earning additional returns. This results in exponential growth, where the returns from the earlier years are reinvested and grow further.

Why Compounding Works in Equity Investments:

- **Reinvestment of Dividends:** Stocks like HDFC Bank and Reliance Industries often pay dividends. If these dividends are reinvested to buy more shares, the investment grows even more. Reinvesting dividends leads to compounding within the investment itself.
- **Capital Appreciation:** As the companies grow, their stock price increases, leading to capital appreciation. This increase in the stock price is compounded over time, enhancing the value of your investment.
- **Consistent Growth:** Stocks from well-managed companies tend to grow consistently over the long term. This steady growth, combined with reinvested dividends, results in compounding that accelerates wealth generation.

The Magic of Compounding in Long-Term Equity Investing:

The real power of compounding becomes evident over longer periods. When you invest in good companies and let your money grow over time, the returns you earn start earning returns themselves. This creates a snowball effect, where the growth accelerates as time goes on.

Key Takeaways:

- **Starting Early:** The earlier you start investing, the more time your money has to compound. Even small investments can grow significantly if given enough time.
- **Consistency is Key:** Regularly adding to your investment, even in small amounts, increases the effect of compounding. This could be in the form of monthly SIPs or reinvestment of dividends.
- **Patience Pays Off:** Compounding rewards patience. The longer you stay invested, the more pronounced the effect of compounding becomes.

"The most powerful force in the universe is compound interest."

—Albert Einstein

Real-World Application of Compounding in Mutual Funds

Mutual funds, especially through **Systematic Investment Plans (SIPs)**, provide an excellent way for Indian investors to harness the power of compounding. SIPs allow individuals to invest a fixed amount regularly, benefiting from the potential growth of the market and the power of compounding. In addition to steady growth, SIPs also leverage the concept of **rupee cost averaging**, which reduces the risk of market volatility.

How SIPs Work:

- **Systematic Investment Plan (SIP):** An SIP is a disciplined way of investing a fixed sum regularly, say ₹5,000 or ₹10,000, in a mutual fund. These small, consistent investments grow over time due to the compounding effect.
- **Rupee Cost Averaging:** In SIPs, you buy more units when the market is low and fewer units when the market is high. This helps average out the cost of the investment over time, mitigating short-term market volatility.
- **Compounding Effect:** The returns generated on your investment also start earning returns, making your money work harder over time. As the corpus grows, the growth accelerates, which is the essence of compounding.

The Power of Long-Term Investing:

The longer you stay invested, the more pronounced the effect of compounding becomes. While it might seem that small, regular contributions won't make a huge difference in the short term, over several years or decades, those small contributions add up, and the returns start multiplying in ways that can result in large sums.

> *"The magic of compounding works best when you invest consistently."*
>
> *—Morgan Housel*

Compounding in Real Estate

Real estate investments also benefit from the power of compounding, though the process takes longer compared to other assets like stocks or mutual funds. In real estate, compounding occurs in two ways: property price appreciation and reinvested rental income. Both contribute to building wealth over time.

How Compounding Works in Real Estate:

- **Property Price Appreciation:** Real estate generally appreciates in value over time. This growth can be relatively steady, driven by factors like location development, increased demand, and infrastructure improvements.
- **Rental Income Reinvestment:** Rental income from properties can be reinvested to purchase additional properties or used to pay down loans, which in turn accelerates wealth accumulation through the compound effect.
- **Long-Term Investment:** While real estate offers compounding, the timeline is longer compared to more liquid investments like stocks or bonds. However,

the potential for significant capital appreciation and consistent cash flow from rental income makes it an attractive option for long-term investors.

Example: Property Price Appreciation

Let's say you purchase a property for ₹30 lakh today. Assuming the property appreciates at an average annual rate of 8%, let's see how the value of your property grows over the next 10 years.

Formula for Compound Growth:

FV = P × (1 + r)^t

Where:

- **FV** = Future Value of the property
- **P** = Initial Price (₹30 lakh)
- **r** = Annual rate of appreciation (8% = 0.08)
- **t** = Number of years (10 years)

Substituting the Values:

FV = 30,00,000 × (1 + 0.08)^10

FV = 30,00,000 × (1.08)^10

FV = 30,00,000 × 2.1589

FV ≈ ₹65,76,700

After 10 years, the property would be worth approximately ₹65.77 lakh, assuming an 8% annual appreciation. This shows how your initial investment grows significantly over time through compounding in the real estate sector.

How Rental Income Compounds:

In addition to capital appreciation, rental income also contributes to compounding. If you receive rental income, you can reinvest it by purchasing more properties, paying down mortgage debt, or improving the property to increase its rental value.

- **Reinvesting Rental Income:** Suppose you receive ₹20,000 per month as rent from the property you purchased for ₹30 lakh. Over time, this rental income can be reinvested into either:
  - Paying off the property loan faster (if you have a loan), reducing interest payments and accelerating equity growth.
  - Purchasing more properties or investing in other asset classes, thus increasing your income-generating assets.
- **Rental Income Growth:** If rent increases over time due to inflation, demand, or property improvements, the income generated also compounds.

Example of Rental Income Reinvestment:

If you reinvest your ₹20,000 monthly rental income into additional real estate, stock markets, or mutual funds, the returns from that reinvestment will compound just like any other investment. Over time, this reinvested capital will also appreciate and generate further wealth.

Key Takeaways:

- **Appreciation and Rent:** The value of the property appreciates over time, and rental income can be reinvested to compound wealth further.
- **Long-Term Horizon:** While compounding in real estate takes longer, the returns are typically higher, especially with reinvested rental income.

- **Leverage the Power of Reinvestment:** Reinvesting rental income or the appreciation of your property allows you to build additional wealth over time.

"The best time to plant a tree was 20 years ago. The second-best time is now."

Patience is Key to Wealth Creation

Building wealth through compounding requires a mindset that is patient, long-term, and disciplined. Compounding works slowly at first but accelerates over time as the interest or returns earned on your initial investment start to generate their own returns. This exponential growth is what makes compounding such a powerful tool for wealth building. However, the key to leveraging this power lies in your ability to **remain patient.**

Why Patience Matters in Compounding

1. **Compounding Takes Time to Gain Momentum**:
    - In the early years of an investment, the returns from compounding may seem small and not very significant. However, as time progresses, these returns begin to snowball, and your wealth grows at an accelerating rate.
    - For example, if you invest ₹10,000 per month in an equity fund earning 12% annually, after 5 years, your corpus will show modest growth. However, after 15 years, the same investment will show significantly higher returns because the compounded amount from previous years continues to grow and generate new returns.

2. **Avoiding Emotional Decisions**:
   - The market can be volatile, with short-term fluctuations that may tempt you to make impulsive decisions, such as selling during market dips. If you focus only on short-term outcomes, it can be easy to lose sight of the long-term goal and disrupt the process of compounding.
   - Patience helps you resist the urge to react emotionally and allows you to stay invested for the long term. The longer you stay invested, the more your returns will compound.
3. **The Power of Consistency**:
   - Consistency in investing is crucial for long-term success. Even small, regular contributions can grow significantly when compounded over time.
   - For instance, if you invest ₹5,000 every month in a mutual fund, you may not see much change in the first few years. But if you keep contributing, over time, the effect of compounding will cause your investment to grow at an accelerating pace.
   - The key is to stay consistent and not get discouraged by the lack of immediate results.

Example of Patience in Wealth Creation:

Let's consider a real-life example to understand how patience works in compounding:

- **Monthly SIP Investment: ₹5,000**
- **Annual Return: 12%**
- **Investment Period: 15 years**

At the start, you are contributing ₹5,000 every month, and initially, the returns will seem modest. But as years go by, your returns start to compound.

- **After 5 years**, your total contributions amount to ₹3 lakh (₹5,000 x 12 months x 5 years), but due to compounding, your investment could have grown to about ₹4.5 lakh.
- **After 10 years**, your total contributions would amount to ₹6 lakh, but the growth through compounding would bring the value to around ₹15 lakh.
- **After 15 years**, you would have contributed ₹9 lakh, but the compounding effect could grow this to over ₹25 lakh.

This shows how, by staying patient and contributing regularly, your wealth grows at an exponential rate as compounding takes effect.

"Patience is the key to success. It's the secret ingredient that turns ordinary into extraordinary."

—Shiv Khera

8

Investing for Tax Savings in India: A Comprehensive Guide

ELSS (Equity Linked Savings Schemes):

- **What It Is:**
  - **Equity Linked Savings Scheme (ELSS)** is a type of mutual fund that primarily invests in stocks (equities) of various companies. These schemes aim to provide capital appreciation over the long term by investing in equity markets. ELSS allows Indian investors to benefit from both high returns and tax savings.
  - It is designed for individuals looking to save taxes while growing their wealth. These funds are actively managed by professional fund managers who invest in equities based on their growth potential.
  - ELSS qualifies for tax-saving purposes under **Section 80C** of the **Income Tax Act**, making it an attractive option for individuals looking to reduce their taxable income while investing in high-growth assets.
- **Tax Benefit:**
  - Investments made in ELSS are eligible for tax deductions under **Section 80C** of the **Income Tax Act** of India.

- Under **Section 80C**, you can claim a tax deduction of up to ₹1.5 lakh per year on investments made in ELSS. This means that by investing in ELSS, you can reduce your taxable income, lowering your overall tax liability.
- For instance, if you invest ₹50,000 in an ELSS fund, your taxable income will reduce by ₹50,000, potentially lowering the taxes you pay for that financial year.

➤ **Lock-In Period:**

- One of the unique features of ELSS is its **lock-in period** of 3 years, which is the shortest among many of the tax-saving instruments available in India, such as the **Public Provident Fund (PPF)** (15 years) and **tax-saving Fixed Deposits** (5 years).
- During the lock-in period, you cannot redeem or withdraw your investment. This ensures that your money stays invested, benefiting from the power of compounding. After 3 years, you can redeem or switch your investments, but long-term investors often hold their ELSS investments for more than 3 years to gain the full benefits of equity market growth.

➤ **Example:**

- Let's say you invest ₹50,000 in an ELSS mutual fund. This investment will allow you to claim ₹50,000 as a tax deduction under **Section 80C** of the Income Tax Act. If your total taxable income for the year is

₹8,00,000, after investing ₹50,000 in ELSS, your taxable income will reduce to ₹7,50,000.

- This reduction in taxable income will result in lower tax payments, depending on your tax slab. By making tax-saving investments in ELSS, you not only reduce your tax burden but also potentially earn returns from the appreciation in equity markets over time.

"The best investment you can make is in yourself, and that includes understanding your taxes."

—Robert T. Kiyosaki

NPS (National Pension System):

- **What It Is:**
  - The **National Pension System (NPS)** is a government-backed retirement savings scheme designed to help individuals save for their retirement. It offers investors a secure and systematic way to build a retirement corpus over time. The scheme is open to all Indian citizens, including self-employed individuals, and is regulated by the **Pension Fund Regulatory and Development Authority (PFRDA)**.
  - NPS allows you to invest in a mix of equity, government bonds, and corporate debt, depending on your risk appetite. The goal of NPS is to provide a regular income post-retirement, making it an attractive option for long-term retirement planning.

- **Tax Benefit:**
  - **Section 80C**: Contributions made to the **NPS** are eligible for tax deductions under **Section 80C** of the **Income Tax Act**. This allows you to reduce your taxable income by up to ₹1.5 lakh per year by contributing to the NPS.
  - **Section 80CCD(1B)**: Additionally, under **Section 80CCD(1B)**, you can claim an extra ₹50,000 in tax deductions specifically for your NPS contributions. This means that you can save a total of ₹2 lakh in taxes (₹1.5 lakh under Section 80C + ₹50,000 under Section 80CCD(1B)) by contributing to NPS.
  - For example, if you invest ₹50,000 in NPS, this amount is eligible for deduction under **Section 80CCD(1B)**, and if you also contribute ₹1.5 lakh to other eligible tax-saving instruments (like PPF, ELSS), you can claim an overall tax deduction of ₹2 lakh.
- **Long-Term Benefits:**
  - The National Pension System is designed to be a long-term retirement savings tool, meaning that your contributions are invested in various assets that can grow over time.
  - The benefit of compounding plays a crucial role in NPS as the money grows over decades, potentially giving you substantial returns by the time you retire.
  - Since the fund is meant for retirement, the idea is that your money will grow steadily due to long-term

compounding, and you'll have a decent retirement corpus to rely on.

- The NPS also provides an option to choose between **Active** and **Auto** investment options, allowing you to customize your portfolio based on your risk profile.

➢ **Example:**

- Let's say you contribute ₹50,000 every year to NPS. Over time, this contribution grows thanks to the power of compounding, and in addition to the ₹50,000 you invested, you also claim a tax deduction for this amount.
- If you make this investment for 10 years, you will not only build a substantial retirement corpus but also enjoy the benefit of tax savings during these years. The tax savings, coupled with the long-term compounding, allow your retirement corpus to grow significantly.
- In addition, if you have other tax-saving investments like **ELSS** or **PPF**, the combined deductions from both NPS and these instruments can lead to considerable tax savings every year.

"Retirement is not about quitting your job. It's about creating passive income that frees you."

—Brian Tracy

PPF (Public Provident Fund):

➢ **What It Is:**

- PPF is a long-term, government-backed savings and investment scheme, designed to offer a secure and tax-free return. It is ideal for conservative investors looking for a low-risk option to build wealth over time.

- It offers **tax benefits** under **Section 80C** of the Income Tax Act, which allows you to claim deductions on contributions made to the fund, up to a maximum of **₹1.5 lakh** in a financial year.

➢ **Tax Benefit:**

- Contributions made to PPF up to **₹1.5 lakh** in a financial year are eligible for **tax deductions** under **Section 80C**.
- The **interest earned** on PPF contributions is **tax-free**, and the maturity amount is also tax-exempt. This makes it a very attractive option for those looking to save on taxes while building a corpus for the future.

➢ **Interest Rate:**

- The **interest rate** on PPF is **set by the Government of India** and is reviewed **quarterly**. The rate can fluctuate depending on market conditions, inflation, and government fiscal policies.
- Historically, the PPF interest rate has ranged from **7.5% to 8%** per annum, but this rate is subject to change every quarter.

For example, the rate might increase or decrease in response to the broader economic environment, and investors need to be aware of such changes as they affect future returns.

- **Lock-In Period:**
  - The lock-in period for **PPF** is **15 years**, which is longer compared to many other tax-saving instruments. This means that you cannot withdraw the invested amount until the completion of this term.
  - However, partial withdrawals are allowed after the **6th year**, which provides some flexibility.
  - After 15 years, the account can be extended in blocks of 5 years, which can also help accumulate additional wealth. But, note that you can only make partial withdrawals or close the account once the lock-in period is complete.
- **Changes in Interest Rates and Regulations:**
  - The **interest rate** on PPF is **set by the government** and reviewed quarterly. While it is generally stable, it can be adjusted based on the prevailing economic conditions, inflation rates, and government fiscal policy. Thus, it's important to stay updated on these changes to anticipate how your returns may fluctuate.
  - **Tax regulations** related to PPF, such as the tax-free status of interest earned and the exemption of the maturity amount from taxes, are currently secured under the **Income Tax Act**, but could be reviewed or modified by the government during the **Union Budget** or other fiscal reforms.
  - Regulatory changes may also affect the rules related to **withdrawals**, **contributions**, and **extensions**. It's important for investors to review these updates

periodically to ensure they are optimizing their investment strategy.

"The goal of investing is to build wealth and secure your financial future. The tax benefits are the added bonus."

—Shiv Khera

Summary of Key Points:

- **Tax Saving:** Contributions up to ₹1.5 lakh in PPF are tax-deductible under Section 80C, and interest earned is tax-free.
- **Interest Rate:** The rate is set by the government and may change quarterly based on economic conditions.
- **Lock-In Period:** The investment is locked for 15 years, but partial withdrawals are allowed after the 6th year.
- **Regulatory Changes:** Interest rates and tax regulations for PPF may change based on government policy, which can impact your returns and the benefits you receive from the instrument.
- **Section 80C Investments:**
  - What It Is: Section 80C of the Income Tax Act allows deductions for a wide range of investments and expenses, including life insurance premiums, ELSS, PPF, NSC (National Savings Certificates), and tuition fees.
  - Tax Benefit: The total tax deduction allowed under Section 80C is up to ₹1.5 lakh.

- Examples of Eligible Investments:
- **Life Insurance Premiums:** Premiums paid for life insurance policies can be claimed under Section 80C.
- **National Savings Certificates (NSC):** These are fixed-income instruments offered by the government and provide both tax benefits and guaranteed returns.
- **5-Year Fixed Deposit:** A tax-saving FD with a 5-year lock-in period qualifies for tax deduction under Section 80C.

"Don't wait for opportunity to knock, create it through intelligent planning and tax-saving strategies."

—Napoleon Hill

- **Tax Saving Fixed Deposits:**
  - What It Is: A tax-saving FD is a fixed deposit with a 5-year lock-in period that qualifies for a tax deduction under Section 80C.
  - Tax Benefit: You can claim deductions of up to ₹1.5 lakh in a financial year under Section 80C for investments in tax-saving FDs.
  - Example: If you invest ₹1 lakh in a tax-saving FD, you can claim a tax deduction for this amount.

"The more you know about taxes and deductions, the more wealth you can create."

—Morgan Housel

- **Sukanya Samriddhi Yojana (SSY):**
  - What It Is: A government-backed savings scheme for the girl child, offering tax benefits and attractive interest rates.
  - Tax Benefit: Contributions to SSY qualify for tax deductions under Section 80C, and the interest earned is also tax-free.
  - Example: If you invest ₹1 lakh in SSY, the entire amount qualifies for a tax deduction under Section 80C, and your child can benefit from tax-free returns when the account matures.

Quote: "The future belongs to those who plan and invest wisely today."

—Shiv Khera

- **Tax Implications of Tax-Saving Investments:**
  - While tax-saving investments reduce your taxable income, it's essential to consider their long-term tax implications.
  - Capital Gains Tax: Some of these instruments (like ELSS and stocks) may be subject to capital gains tax when sold, while others like PPF and NSC offer tax-free returns.
  - Example: If you sell your ELSS investment after 3 years, the gains are taxed at 10% (long-term capital gains tax).

"Tax planning is essential for building wealth. Don't let taxes erode your returns."

—Robert T. Kiyosaki

- **Maximizing Tax Savings with Strategic Investments:**
  - Diversify: To maximize tax savings, it's essential to diversify your investments across different tax-saving instruments. This spreads your risk and increases your overall returns.
  - Example: Combining investments in PPF, ELSS, and NPS allows you to reduce your taxable income while building wealth in both conservative and growth-oriented assets.

"Diversification is the only free lunch in investing."

—Nobel laureate Harry Markowitz